Nic and Sue

You do great

work for the Party and Sue m,

and I an so gratful

[signature]
28 ix 2018

FULL ENGLISH
BREXIT

FULL ENGLISH
BREXIT

THE MOST IMPORTANT DEAL OF THE DAY
HOW DO YOU LIKE YOURS?

James Gray MP

HALSGROVE

First published in Great Britain in 2018

British Library Cataloguing-in-Publication Data
A CIP record for this title is available from the British Library

ISBN 978 0 85704 331 3

HALSGROVE
Halsgrove House,
Ryelands Business Park,
Bagley Road, Wellington, Somerset TA21 9PZ
Tel: 01823 653777   Fax: 01823 216796
email: sales@halsgrove.com

Part of the Halsgrove group of companies
Information on all Halsgrove titles is available at: www.halsgrove.com

Printed and bound by Parksons Graphics, India

Contents

Introduction

As a Scot, nothing gets my goat more than people using the word 'English' when they mean 'British.' 'Queen of England' is the commonest. She is not. She is Queen of the United Kingdom of Great Britain and Northern Ireland (including the Isle of Man, Berwick-upon Tweed which allegedly got itself separated from the rest of the UK at some stage in history, of the British Overseas Territories, of much of the Commonwealth and of the Channel Islands).

So the title of this book *Full English Brexit* is a misnomer which the more rabid of my fellow Scots will leap onto 'like a tramp on a kipper'. "Aha!" they will argue. "That proves that even the most ardent Brexiteer (yours truly) accepts it as possible that Scotland will not leave the EU when England does", or some other such banal idiocy.

Well, I am sorry to disappoint you, but the title of this book is little more than a euphonius pun. My cover, which is a November 2016 birthday card drawn for me by my daughter Olivia, was its inspiration, offering as it does a full menu of EU Breakfasts. (And don't be misled by the 'Or MAYbe never' cartoon, which was drawn during the Supreme Court hearing into Article 50 and whether or not it needed a Parliamentary motion. Hence the three bewigged judges/chefs in the top right hand corner.)

'Full British Brexit' or 'Full UK Brexit' would just not have caught the imagination in quite the same way. So *Full English Brexit* it is. But pace the Scottish National Party, it refers to the whole of the UK. (Incidentally Northern Ireland is not part of Great Britain either, yet the Province will just as assuredly be in 'Brexit' as any other part of the United Kingdom.)

My second apology is to those who might have bought this book in the hope that it would be some kind of a re-run of the Brexit Referendum campaign. They are like the man with the sore tooth. Europhiles and Brexiteers alike just can't leave it alone. They re-fight the old fights, remind everyone what they had to say in those glory days before the Referendum. They're the old bores sipping pink gins in the corner of the Officers' Mess recounting tales from their war (very probably drawing a veil over the fact that they were in reality only the junior officer in charge of pink gin in the Mess long after the fighting was over.)

We must, unlike them, now put the substantive arguments about Brexit behind us. The people spoke in the Referendum. They mandated the Government to withdraw from the EU. That is what we are now doing – irrevocably after the delivery of the Article 50 letter. There are no 'ifs', no 'buts.' No hard Brexit or soft Brexit, no red, white and blue Brexit. The fact is that at 11pm on 30 March 2019, the UK will leave the EU. All that is left is to decide the method of our going, and the terms of the post-divorce relationship with the remaining EU countries and with the EU itself (which is by no means the same thing.)

So this book is not about England (it's about the whole of the UK); it's not about Brexit (or at least not mainly – we are all a bit bored by Brexit.) And it's not about Breakfast either (in case through any mischance any lover of two sausages and a fried egg bought the book looking for recipes). It's not even about being 'Full' so much as being 'Great'.

It is intended to be about what made Britain Great; and about what post-Brexit we must do to make us Great again (unlike Donald Trump's idle boast about making America 'Great again', at least we have 'Great' in our name.) It's about what we want Britain to look like, what kind of Britain we want to pass to subsequent generations. It's about what we can do both in and for the world. It's about power through Aid and War; it's about Britain as a great trading nation, about our Parliament and laws, about our diplomatic, cultural and ethical contribution to the wider world.

In other words, it's an attempt at some kind of strategic rethink about who we are, what we are for. It is intensely personal, deliberately controversial, I hope thought-provoking in parts. And if it provides some little stimulus to a much wider debate, then it will have done its job.

I am indebted to a great many people who have been of huge help in compiling this mildly encyclopaedic work. My Parliamentary Chief of Staff, that most British of all Slovakians, Adam Fico runs a large part of my political and professional life and had a hand in many aspects of the book, as did my Private Secretary, Amy Swash. Duncan Depledge, who has played a leading role in reviving Parliament's knowledge and understanding of the Polar Regions is largely responsible for that chapter. Fred de Fossard, whose academic prowess currently labours in the Parliamentary Resources Unit, has a great writing future ahead of him, and provided much of the inspiration for the chapter on Britain's diplomatic future. My Military Chief of Staff, Johnny Longbottom has kept the Armed Forces Parliamentary Scheme going, and advised me on military matters. Ross Crapnell proof-read it and avoided a host of infelicities (and spelling and grammatical errors). And my wife, Philippa, has tolerated long hours in my study, and made a myriad contributions throughout the book. The publishers, Halsgrove in Wellington, Somerset, so ably led by Steven Pugsley have been an inspiration and help throughout, and will, I hope, be ready to publish some more of my scribblings in the future. None of them bear any responsibility for the views I express, many of which are personal and controversial. They have all been magnanimous in suppressing their own, sometimes sharply divergent thoughts.

1. A Great Moment in History

"History will be kind to me, for I intend to write it."
(Winston Churchill)

There are moments in the history of any nation or civilisation in which an action, or lack of it, defines the history of that nation for generations to come. Whatever it is, it sets a clear (perhaps only in retrospect) direction of travel. 9/11 was one such; so was 7/7; so was the Brexit referendum on 23 June 2016. Historians will rank those events alongside some of the great iconic moments of history, and will ponder in particular whether subsequent developments would, or could, have been different if only we had known what a turning point in our history the event in question was. This time – Britain's Exit from the EU, Brexit – we do know, and we have a unique opportunity to fashion our collective future as a result. If only we grasp that opportunity.

It was not always so. Most way-points in the world's history have come and gone without contemporary commentators realising their significance. When Julius Caesar shielded his eyes against the setting sun, looked over the Channel at the White Cliffs of Dover, and declared *'Veni, Vidi, Vici'* in 55 BC (although he was in historical fact referring to his Victory at the Battle of Zela against Pharnaces ll of Pontus), he may well have been cross, resentful or disappointed to have been despatched to this bleak and unknown outpost of Empire. He may well have hankered for the luxuries of Rome. What he certainly did not know was that his arrival on these shores, and Rome's final departure 465 years later in 410 AD, started the process of civilisation on which so much of modern British history and culture is based.

Even more startlingly, Christopher Columbus's accidental discovery of America, he having set off to find a route to the East Indies in search of untold wealth in spices and silks for his Spanish employers and sponsors, created the crucible from which the greatest superpower of our time, America, was born. He was Genoese, but his chance discovery had immense consequences for the subsequent history of Great Britain.

Richard Arkwright's invention of the Spinning Jenny in 1769, James Watt's invention of the steam engine two years later; Robert Stephenson's *Rocket* in 1829, and so many other almost incidental inventions meant that in the space of no more than fifty years we went from rural peace and certainty to industrial revolution and urbanisation and a world which few people can have imagined or planned for. Our cities grew at an alarming rate; our countryside and way of life changed for ever. And the economic and industrial foundations were laid for the largest and greatest Empire the world has ever seen. But did Watt and Stephenson and Arkwright really know the consequences of their inventions? Did Sir Tim Berners-Lee know that his creation of the Worldwide Web would revolutionise the way of life of virtually every human being on the Globe? I suspect that none of them did.

(About 1982, as a young shipbroker, I was approached by a man who wanted to charter an extremely rare and expensive cable-laying vessel 'to link,' he said, 'all of the Continents by undersea cable so that all of the computers in the world could speak to one another in something to be called the World Wide Web.' Well, I can spot a mad man at a thousand paces, so I showed him the door suggesting he should not waste my time with such nonsense!)

Of course, we do now know the long-term consequences of Hannibal crossing the Alps with his elephants, of William of Normandy setting sail for Hastings; of Gavrilo Princip taking a pot shot at the Archduke Franz Ferdinand in Sarajevo in 1914. We do now know that the entire recent history of the Middle East – and the West's disastrous entanglements in Iraq and Afghanistan – became inevitable from the moment that some obscure US flying instructor trained the 9/11 suicide pilots to fly. But did they know it? Of course not.

Few of us know what the day will bring when we get out of bed in the morning, far less what long-term consequences it may have. Few, if any, people, at the time recognise the significance of whatever it is they are doing. If they were better equipped to do so, then their ability to shape their own, their nation's and the world's future would be transformed.

Yet alongside those accidental, or incidental, historic events, there are other occasions when from a behind a preset plan can be discerned truly great thinking. These are occasions in history where players really do have a vision, and take actions, often against huge opposition, to make that dream a reality. Ghenghis Khan must have had such a dream – domination of a vast empire. Perhaps some of the great explorers and missionaries – David Livingston, Scott of the Antarctic, Marco Polo – did so. Perhaps a few of the greatest statesmen and political visionaries – Burke, Disraeli, Churchill (or at least he said he did), Thatcher – did so too. Were they giants amongst men, whose magnificent long-term vision of the future of our Nation created it? Or were they too products of the broad flow of history? Did they make history, or were they just the right person in the right place at the right time? Of such discussions is the very stuff of the study of history itself.

The great tides of history, whether caused by accidental, or inadvertent events, or by great men with great strategic vision taking decisive action, have one – perhaps obvious – thing in common. Great events in history tend to occur when history is adrift, when there is weakness, uncertainty, chaos, in world affairs.

The Saxon Kings of England were blissfully unaware at Stamford Bridge in 1066 of what was about to hit them; wholly unconscious that the Normans were to wreak such havoc and then so fundamentally to change English history and culture as they would do within a few months.

King Harold's death by an arrow in the eye, Bayeux Tapestry.

It is interesting to note that one of the reason's for the Norman victory at Hastings was because they had discovered the use of stirrups which enable you to thrust and cut on horseback. The Saxons did not have that advantage, and so dismounted and fought from the ground as this little slice of the Bayeux Tapestry so clearly shows.

The Second World War was a product of the poverty, collapse and weakness of the interwar years across Europe, and of industrial disputes and economic collapse. Nazism took advantage of that chaos, unhappiness and political vacuity. ISIS (or Daesh as I prefer to call that wicked bunch of murderers) struck decisively in the turmoil caused by civil war in Syria, the end of the dictator Gaddafi in Libya, the chaotic vacuum left by the West in Iraq, Civil War in the Yemen and the resurgence of the Taliban in Afghanistan and Pakistan amongst many other elements creating chaos in the whole region stretching from Tunisia to Iran; from Pakistan to the Ukraine; from Egypt to Kazakhstan.

Nature abhors a vacuum it is said, and it is into a vacuum or historic chaos, which is often the corollary of it, that an event happens that can shape the entire future of a country, or a continent or a civilisation. Brexit, Trump, Syria, an expansionist Russia – now is exactly that moment of historical vortex, or vacuum, into which people with real vision can stride and shape the future for 100 – or 1000 – years to come. Now is our moment. Now is the time when vision, determination, historical perspective, can truly have an effect for generations to follow.

That is why we need some real and fundamental thinking about where we are in the great sweep of history; what it is that is happening around us; and what we – here in Britain – can now do to shape the world's future. The question we are trying to answer is: Post-Brexit who are we as a Nation, and what are we for? What is our role in the world and in history? Do we have a clear direction? Are we flotsam floating around on the tides of history, or are we as a Nation helping to make it? Are we content just to potter along in rather a British sort of way waiting to see what is in store for us just around the corner? Or are we ready to project our power in the world, fight for what we know to be true and good and just; oppose cruelties and dictatorships; mend ignorance and poverty, starvation and sickness wherever it may be?

Now is the time for some grand strategic thinking. It is hoped that this book may make some little contribution to that great generational debate.

So let's give it a shot.

2. The Perfect Storm

"A detrimental or calamitous situation arising from the powerful combined effect of a unique set of circumstances." (OED)

The World stands on the edge of a perfect storm. It's a storm which threatens the lives, prosperity, freedoms, of our children and grandchildren. It's a storm of Millenarian, of Old Testament proportions. Yet it's a storm which few people have so far realised or anticipated. And it's a storm which the world is ill-equipped to withstand, far less to reverse.

Its elements are diverse and interconnected, and they range from the global and generational to the local and temporary. If even some parts of them coincide, that woefully pessimistic group of doom-saying economists, the Limits to Growth group, may well come to look like naïve and over-enthusiastic optimists.

Just allow yourself a quick *tour d'horizon.*

That some form of climate change exists seems now to be accepted even by the most rabid of sceptics, although some (Lord Lawson, Mr Trump), maintain a healthy debate about its causes and solutions. Leaving them aside, the reality is that the Arctic ice is disappearing at an alarming rate, its withdrawal becoming something of a self-fulfilling prophesy. Weather patterns across the globe are being regularly disrupted with floods, hurricanes, earthquakes, droughts, freezing and heatwaves becoming the norm, and 1000 year events occurring once a decade. The consequences of unchecked Global Warming could alone be catastrophic within a few years.

Lyell Glacier in the Yosemite National Park 130 years apart.

Climate change is linked – causally and consequentially – to many of the other elements of our Perfect Storm.

The world's economy, having only just started to recover from the banking collapse of 2008, now faces a series of likely shocks.

Commodity production and consequent pricing holds some elements of catastrophe. $50 oil as a result of overproduction by Russia and Saudi and in reaction to the development of shale gas and fracking, especially in the United States, has dramatic consequences for the whole of the Middle East; for an unstable and sanction-crippled Russia; for Nigeria (shortly to become the third most populous country in the world) and parts of West and North Africa; and for Venezuela and Central America. The historic importance and stabilising influence of OPEC has been much diminished both by new producers and by alternative fuels. So the days of Saudi Arabia turning off a few taps to stabilise the oil price are long gone.

The over dominance of China in so many markets has worrying consequences for the West. The flooding of Europe with over-produced Chinese steel (4918 tonnes in February 1990 had become 72,231 tonnes by June 2017) has disastrous results for the basic lifeblood of Western manufacturing capability: steel production.

Shrewd Chinese investment promises a stranglehold in so many other areas of the world's economy. Take one example – rare earths. These are seventeen elements in the periodic table (such as Scandium, Yttrium, Praseodymium), which are used for a wide variety of industrial purposes, including every single computer and mobile phone in existence. Yet 95% of the world's rare earths are mined in China. A large part of the balance is in Greenland, where recent developments look like allowing 3000 Chinese labourers to develop mines there. A global Chinese monopoly on the refining and production of rare earths has terrifying implications for the rest of the World. Chinese ownership of Western bonds and debt, and her influence over the world's currency markets has not yet been fully felt. China has traded the World's money markets pretty responsibly in recent years realising that they alone could destabilise bond and currency markets as well as stock markets to such an extent that they would destroy their own wealth. But can we always rely on their economic and financial sophistication and self-control? China owns $1.8 trillion of US Bonds, some 8%; and they are known to own a fair part of the 30% of UK debt which is held overseas, and of Euro debt as well (the ownership of which is not announced with a curious lack of transparency).

Even more toxic for Europe than all of that must be the migrant crisis. Instability, poverty and wars throughout the Middle East and North and Central Africa makes the prospect of even a deeply hazardous overland trip to Europe enormously attractive with its prosperity, jobs, education, welfare, health care, a moderate climate, decent housing and modern transport systems. Until the invention of the Internet none of the West's massive and disproportionate wealth was known to many ordinary people throughout most of the developing world. But now, at the stroke of a mouse, it is possible for all to see our cars and deep freezes, our flat screen TVs, water on tap, education, health and obesity. How most ordinary people in the rest of the world must crave for so many of the things which we take for granted.

Whose heart did not break at that photograph a couple of years ago of the innocent little three-year-old boy in his smart red tee shirt, blue shorts and trainers lying dead face down on a beach in Turkey? Like the little Polish boy with his hands up in the Warsaw Ghetto, or the crying burned child from the Vietnam War – these are

Bodrum, Turkey.

appalling heart-rending icons of a cry for help. The dreadful deaths of migrants in the Mediterranean, the squalor of the former Jungle Camp in Calais, the chaos in Budapest – all of these things are but symptoms of a much wider malaise.

We are witnessing the largest mass migration of peoples in the history of the world. Behind it lies warfare in Syria, Libya, Iraq and Afghanistan; terrorism across much of the northern half of Africa as well as the Middle East; the Israeli/Palestinian conflict; poverty across half the globe (while the other half suffers from obesity); the pernicious effects of people using religion as a cover for their own greedy, violent, demented ends. These are influences predicted by the

Warsaw, Poland.

Vietnam.

Willy Brandt Report thirty-five years ago. They are now taking place.

The absurd EU Schengen agreement means that once through some of its more or less porous borders, travel is pretty uninterrupted across the Continent. (And the Eire/Northern Ireland border looks like remaining 'open' after Brexit, which will surely be an open invitation to the world's dispossessed.) The vastness of the black economy means that a pretty good life can be hacked out of the soil by illegal migrants without the necessity of becoming known to the authorities. (Vastly better at all events than a peasant or war-torn existence in Africa or the Middle East.) So the migrant crisis is with us for keeps. It is a human tide the like of which the world has never seen.

I absolutely agree with all of my constituency correspondents who say that "we must do something about it." But I also have every sympathy with those who reply "Yes, but what?" Half of my constituency mailbag is full of letters of outrage at the very high immigration figures, demanding that we should close our doors to migrants, arguing that we have neither the space nor the resources to house them. Half of my constituents want to see compassionate immigration; the other half want to see the drawbridge pulled up at Calais.

My own view is that we must try to differentiate between economic migrants (the Dick Whittingtons of the twenty-first century), genuine political asylum seekers like the Afghan interpreters who face imprisonment or death at home thanks to their service to the British Government; and the millions of refugees displaced from their homes and their homelands by warfare and persecution. How you differentiate amongst the different categories, each of which is worthy of a different level and type of help, is anyone's guess, especially when they are all jumbled up in migration camps across Europe.

I very much welcome that we in Britain have taken 20,000 or so refugees from the camps on the border of war-torn Syria, and that we have already provided over £900 million in aid for those fleeing war in Syria and Iraq. This is more than any other European country. But there isn't a solution to this problem that is simply about taking people. Simply throwing open our doors, as some have suggested we should do out of compassion, and very much as Angela Merkel did in Germany, would solve really very little. Indeed it might make things worse since it would be saying to the remaining people in Syria, Libya, Iraq, Afghanistan and elsewhere "make your way to the borders of Europe and we will give you shelter."

So we must be compassionate. We must find a way to help these poor people whose lives have been destroyed by warfare at home. We must give political asylum to true asylum seekers, but we must filter out the fakes and economic migrants, and violent terrorists who may well be hiding amongst them. And at the same time as all of that, we must – by overseas aid or military means – try to establish peace and security in their homelands. We must police the vicious thugs who are trafficking them, and we must seek to rebalance the world's inequalities of food and water and economic resources. If you fancy that job then you're a braver person than me.

But the poor little boy in his best outfit dead on the beach in Turkey is an image which will last forever, and which prompts Winston Churchill's great cry "Action this day".

Climate change whose consequences cannot readily be foretold, world economic instability and the commodity price collapse, political uncertainty in the US, UK and EU, the migrant crisis – these elements alone constitute a pretty imminent storm. And that is without even thinking about geopolitical developments across the rest of the world.

The US and Britain's military adventures in Iraq, Afghanistan and Libya, may well all have been justifiable one way or another in their own rights, and in the aftermath of 9/11. Or at least we thought that they were at the time. Yet the removal of dictators in Iraq and Libya, and of a totalitarian Taliban regime in Afghanistan coupled with a seven-year bloody civil war in Syria have all left a huge political vacuum at the heart of the Middle East and North Africa into which Daesh, Al Nusra, AQAP, Kurdish terrorists and a host of gangsters of one sort or another have hurried. The end result of fifteen years of bloodshed in Iraq and Afghanistan is that those countries and the entire region are significantly worse off in many ways than they would have been had we done nothing.

I am equally (and uncharacteristically) in two minds about what more we should be doing in Syria. It is perfectly logical and sensible that if Daesh are our enemies (which of course is beyond doubt), we should bomb them at their head-quarters around Raqqa in Syria. That is why I voted for that action in Parliament in 2016 despite my concerns that our eight Tornado aircraft would have very little effect, and that the whole region is becoming a wholly unpredictable maelstrom.

Russia, Iran, Hezbollah, and perhaps even China are supporting President Assad with overwhelming military might against the moderate Syrian rebels, who have been armed and trained to a degree by the West. They are also targeting Daesh. Is our enemy's enemy automatically our friend? Should we overlook the situation in the Ukraine and Crimea for pragmatic reasons? Should we rattle sabres in the Baltic States if President Putin is to be our new best friend? Can we overlook Assad's Hitler-style dictatorship, his slaughtering of hundreds of thousands of his own people and that he has caused millions to flee their homes? Can we overlook Russian planes in NATO airspace over Turkey in favour of defeating Daesh? The whole thing is a mess and the consequences of doing the wrong thing are, I believe, potentially profound.

A resurgent Russia meanwhile has invaded Crimea and Eastern Ukraine – both actions outlawed by the UN. President Putin is widely presumed to be considering what action he can or should take in the Baltic states – Estonia, Latvia and Lithuania. They have large Russian populations, were part of the USSR, and block Russia's access to their Baltic enclave, the most heavily militarised zone in the world, Kaliningrad. How Mr Putin must wish he could simply annex them. The Zapad 2017, 100,000 troop, Russian Exercise only a few hundred miles from the NATO/EU border is seen by some to be a possible rehearsal for some kind of intervention in Poland or the Baltic States. But the Baltic States are different to Crimea. They are members of NATO, Article 5 of whose Treaty swears that foreign aggression against any one member is deemed to be against us all; and also of the EU. Would we really tolerate a Ukrainian-style attack, even a partial, deniable or covert one on part of NATO and the EU? Surely not.

North Korea, meanwhile, a nation whose economy is only one fiftieth as big as that of its democratic capitalist cousin, South Korea, whose GDP is half the amount Americans spend on their pets, a backward and eccentric little dictatorship, is – despite recent diplomatic developments – nonetheless threatening the US and the world with apparently more or less viable Intercontinental Ballistic Missiles with miniaturised nuclear warheads. The risk of inadvertent escalation, or of simple error by either side, or by an understandably nervous South Korea, is very grave.

Add to all of that, political and military chaos in North Africa as a whole, probable civil war and economic collapse in Venezuela and tensions in the South China Sea. Throw into the melting pot the little-known world of cyber warfare, using which an enemy could at the stroke of a few computer keys paralyse large parts of the West, and save room for the increasing likelihood of terrorists using 'dirty bombs' of one kind or another, and you have the outline of a very toxic mix indeed.

As if that were not enough, the geopolitical mayhem is exacerbated by the poverty, starvation, thirst, drought, famine and chaos caused by them throughout much of the developing world. Remember Willi Brandt's prescient report on the global North/South divide fifty years ago? Add the climatic effects of Global Warming, the retreating Arctic ice-cap, or at very least the global effects of El Nino and his sister El Nina, and you have a perfect physical and environmental storm so intimately linked in many ways with the simultaneous geopolitical and military perfect storm we face. The gathering dark clouds of climate change and commodity and economic turbulence are blowing across a world on the edge of structural collapse. The United States will be increasingly paralysed as, despite the Republican Party's dominance of both Senate and House of Representatives, the 'checks and balances' progressively paralyse and stultify the Trump Administration, whose very unpredictability sorely worsens that sense of global crisis.

The Middle East and North Africa; the Indian sub-Continent and Asia Minor; the South China Sea; European turmoil and the cyber threat; weather and climatic disruption; poverty, starvation and thirst, one billion people going to bed starving as another billion sleep obese. If I felt that, rather than a perfect storm, this was some kind of a temporary worry; and that we could confidently look forward to every Beauty Pageant Queen's one wish – "World Peace" – then I might have hesitated about writing this book. My fears would have disappeared and my writings rendered out of date.

I fear, however, that that is extremely unlikely. The details may well change, and change significantly. But I am confident in predicting that no matter how much after 2018 you are reading this, the world will be just as dangerous and messy a place. The details may well change but the risks will be timeless. And the need to know what role we in Britain will take in that mayhem, that toxic mess, will be as important in 2028 and 2038 as it is in 2018. The world is a more confusing and dangerous place than it has been for many generations. It is chaos, a vacuum of the worst kind – which is precisely the atmosphere into which an event or a strong personality can come to wreak havoc and re-polarise the history of the world.

The world is indeed facing a Perfect Storm.

3. 23 June 2016

*"If Britain must choose between Europe and the open sea,
she must always choose the open sea…"* (Winston Churchill)

Into that Perfect Storm comes Brexit. That something massive, tectonic, history-shaping, generational, happened on Thursday 23 June, 2016 (when the British people voted to leave the European Union) is obvious. Much harder – nay probably impossible – is to be clear about what happened, nor why, nor its short, medium or long term consequences for Britain (clearly), for Europe (without a doubt) and therefore very probably for the world as a whole.

The 'Remain' camp had predicted catastrophe if we left the EU. They forecasted a collapsing Stock Exchange (as I write it is trading at record high levels), a disaster for the pound (ignoring the fact that a slightly weaker pound is actually very beneficial for exports, and therefore overall of benefit to the economy as a whole); and they promised an 'Emergency Budget' to stave off an economic collapse equal in severity to the slump in 1920s America (yet the Governor of the Bank of England who had been one of the greatest nay-sayers now seems to believe that Brexit is perfectly manageable). They anticipated a quasi-racist, neo-Nazi eviction of all non-UK passport holders (blithely ignoring the fact that industries like health, long-term care, catering, building and plumbing all depend for their very survival on workers from overseas). The then Chancellor of the Exchequer, (of less than blessed memory) George Osborne, rather bizarrely claimed that house prices "will dive by 18% if we leave." It is hard to know how anyone could make such an exact prediction. And anyhow, restraining the prices of houses is something which the very same Chancellor separately espoused to help first time buyers. The end result, of course, is that house prices are pretty much as strong post-referendum as they were before it. The only things the gloom-mongers in the Remain camp failed to predict as a consequence of a vote to leave was Armageddon, a plague of frogs and the death of the first-born (although some of them came very close to it on various occasions). President of the EU, Donald Tusk, for example, famously opined "As a historian, I fear that Brexit could be the beginning of the destruction of not only the EU but also Western political civilisation in its entirety." Enough said…

BRITAIN STRONGER IN EUROPE

This is not the place for a Brexit campaign post-mortem. But history will record that the Remain campaign (fetchingly called Britain Stronger in Europe, or BSE for short, ignoring the coincidence of name with Bovine Spongiform

Encepalopathy, BSE, or mad-cow disease) was a disaster. Stretch your mind back to the £9 million spent issuing a dreary document of 'facts' to each household which was both too early to have much effect, and widely perceived as blatant Government propaganda, and therefore self-defeating. Recall No 10 issuing President Obama with a 'line to take', including the uniquely British expression "end of the queue" (an American would have said "back of the line"). These and a hundred other bloomers threw their campaign away.

Brexit protest.

Prime Minister David Cameron mishandled the whole episode. He it was who allowed the referendum to be included in the Conservative Party Manifesto in the first place, presumably in the sure and certain hope that rather than a majority government we would have another coalition with the Liberal Democrats who would never allow such a referendum to take place. He then mishandled the 'negotiation' with Europe, and the subsequent Referendum campaign itself, fatally besmirching his own name and securing his legacy as 'the PM who fouled up over Europe.' (Blair foundered over Iraq, Maggie Thatcher over local government finance, Churchill was bizarrely punished for winning the War. As Enoch Powell once famously observed 'All political careers end in failure.')

The Leave campaign, by contrast, was well planned and executed, and appealed to a range of people over a diversity of issues. It drew those with a general dislike of Brussels and an intuitive longing to regain our Sovereignty (amongst Tory voters in the South of England), those with a hatred of 'immigration' and a longing to regain control of our borders (in East Anglia, Yorkshire and the North); those with a dislike of the Tory Government and David Cameron (in the Labour heartlands everywhere); and those with a general dissatisfaction with the political establishment, and a longing to 'give them all a good kicking.' A similar dislike of the political status quo has led to an upswing in nationalism across Europe, and the Donald Trump Presidency in the United States. The disaffected blue collar workers in Marseille, Milwaukee and Middlesbrough have been sending our politicians a powerful message which we ignore at our peril.

There can be all kinds of criticisms levelled at both camps ('lies, distortions, exaggeration'), but only one thing really matters. On 23 June, 2016 the people of Britain in a perfectly well-run and internationally accepted Referendum, voted to leave the European Union. That is all there is to it. That is that. We will come out at 11pm on 31st March, 2019 (two years to the day after triggering Article 50) and there is nothing that anyone can do about it. We will have left the great behemoth in the sky. That cannot – and if you believe in democracy must not – be reversed. There will be no second referendum, no renegotiation, no 'soft landing.' The people have spoken, and we must accept it and just get on with it.

There is no such thing as a 'hard' Brexit, nor a 'soft' one, nor a 'red white and blue one,' nor anything in between. Either we are In the EU or we are Out of it. The 'Hard Brexit' name has been devised by the Remain camp to frighten the electorate into thinking that if we leave we are facing poverty, job losses, and general catastrophe.

Of course, there are details which must be negotiated and agreed.

For example, we need the 3.8 million EU workers currently in the UK, just as they need the roughly 1 million Brits working in the EU, alongside large numbers of retired British people. All of that should not be hard to sort out. Everyone who is in the UK on the day we leave must be allowed to stay; those who have lived here for five years or more will essentially get indefinite leave to remain. Thereafter, we will of course want migrant workers – fulfilling essential jobs in agriculture, the NHS, long-term care, the construction industry – to continue to come here. It would be crazy not to do so. But it should be for the UK Government to decide how many are allowed to come in. We will at last have the ability to prevent the 750 million people across the Continent from flooding into the UK at their will, and by right of their citizenship of any one of the 28 EU countries.

Immigration is one of the least understood, or perhaps most deliberately misunderstood, of all current political debates. And it leads to some of the bitterest and most unacceptable of all political diatribes.

It is my strongly held view that a human being is a human being. Young or old, male or female, rich or poor, white, black or indifferent. We are all one humanity. Racism, sexism, ageism or any other 'ism' including snobbery and inverted snobbery are anathema to me. People should treat other people with grace and courtesy no matter who they may be.

"A man's a man for all that," as Robbie Burns said. Yet what he did not say is: *"A person, irrespective of their race or ethnicity, their religious beliefs, their sexual orientation or lack of one, their material or intellectual assets..."* You get the kind of thing I mean. Sometimes we are so desperately keen to show that we are not racist nor snobbish that we fall over ourselves in the opposite direction into absurd and self-regarding political correctness. I, for example, happen to believe that men and women are different; that there is nothing wrong with standing up for Britain and British people (of all races); and that we celebrate Christmas in a Christian country because that was when Christ was born.

We can respect people of all kinds without self-righteously thrusting down their throats that that is what we are doing. To do so reflects more on ourselves than on the person to whom we are showing due respect despite or because of their race or ethnicity.

So I fully subscribe to the view that our British infrastructure is already over-stretched. We are, for example, the most densely packed country in Europe after Malta. We do not have room, jobs, school places, housing, to welcome the world's poor to our doors. It is right and proper that we restrict immigration to those people who we want to come here. And there are plenty of them. Large parts of the NHS, long-term care, catering, building, agriculture, would collapse were it not for overseas workers of all kinds in this country. I welcome immigration. But it must be in categories that we set. We simply cannot allow the 750 million people across the EU who currently have a perfect right to come here, to do so.

So of course we have to find ways of getting it under control; it is perfectly reasonable to say that we prefer British people to be carrying out British jobs where that can be done. It would be absurd not to do so. But to interpret that perfectly reasonable patriotic vision as Xenophobia or racism is to fall into precisely the politically correct trap which I describe.

I am in no sense a racist, a sexist, nor a xenophobe. But I am clear that we in Britain should be the ones who decide who else should come to join us on these little islands. Let us encourage immigration where it is needed. But let us control it. And if mad or bad people choose to use that determination as camouflage to espouse racism, then they must be stopped, and they must be punished for it. Racism, after all, is already against the law. And quite right too.

Patriotism is a love of one's country. Nationalism is a hatred of everyone else's.

There are other elements of the EU legacy which we must embrace. Worthwhile EU laws, for example, on the environment, and protecting workers rights, will be transferred en masse onto the UK Statute Book, alongside the 20,000 or so EU laws which currently exist. The entire corpus of European law will become part of the UK Statute Book on the day we leave, and we can then repeal or change bits of it as we wish over the coming years. That will be at the will of the British people, and decided in the UK Parliament at Westminster.

Trade will at last be a matter for us. How can it be that a great trading and maritime nation such as ours are not allowed to make trade deals round the world? Why can we not be members of the World Trade Organisation ourselves? Why should we be prevented from a trade agreement with the US, for example? As for trade within the EU? Well more comes this way than goes that way, so it really should not be a problem for that to continue. We don't need to be members of the Single Market, nor Customs Union, which in reality prevent proper trading relationships with the rest of the world.

There will be a financial divorce settlement, in which we will get rid of our shares in the buildings, pay off long-term employees, sort out pension funds and so on. That is what happens, for example, when two companies de-merge. We must pay our liabilities. Of course we must. But just like a divorce settlement, neither side must be allowed to 'take the other to the cleaners'. The notion, for example, that we must pay until the completion of infrastructure projects to which we were party when a member of the EU is absurd. It may well be that while we were a member of it the EU Commission agreed to road projects in Romania, tobacco farming in Italy, or massive investment in the Arctic, and in 'Embassies' across the Globe. But that by no means justifies our having to pay for those projects indefinitely. Their lack of accountability is one of the very reasons why we are leaving.

So let's stop worrying about it. We are leaving the EU. There are all sorts of bits and pieces to be sorted out, none of them insuperable. And above all let's get away from the utter drivel being spouted by some of those who would like to overturn the will of the people, either by staying 'in', or even worse making some kind of Machiavellian plot the end result of which would be all the worst bits of the EU, with none of the benefits. Let's have a clean break, and get on with deciding our own futures.

Pundits, professors and bar-room bores can speculate till the cows come home what the consequences will be. But in the meantime those arch-Brexiteers, Boris Johnson, David Davis and Liam Fox have been set the task, supported by an army of the brightest and best of the British civil service, to set about making it happen on the most advantageous terms for the people of Britain. Most observers agree that under the firm hand of Mutter May we will secure our freedom from Mutter Merkel and that we will go our merry way as a free and independent Nation State. We will be run not from Brussels but from Parliament in Westminster and by our magnificent (and by comparison with the bloated Brussels bureaucrats, 10,000 of whom earn more than the UK Prime Minister) slim and business-like civil service down Whitehall. For good or ill we will be making our own decisions about our own islands. Our elected politicians will stand or fall by the decisions they take in our own Parliament. As a nation we will be truly masters of our own destiny.

That is not to say, however that we are seeking some kind of divorce from the Continent of Europe or from its peoples. I am a strong supporter of Twinning arrangements which are now so universal. Person to person links and community to community friendships are so much better than supranational organisations, most of which are fundamentally flawed. Civilisation and international peace depend on understanding and enjoying other people's way of life and culture, without being asked to adopt them for ourselves.

At a recent Twinning event, for example, between Box in my constituency and Sorigny, I much enjoyed the rather stirring singing of La Marseillaise as the French flag fluttered over the Box Pavilion with its stirring chorus *"Aux armes, citoyens! Formez vos bataillons! Marchons! Marchons! Qu'un sang impur. Abreuve nos sillons!"*

Very French. Perhaps a little too republican and revolutionary for my personal tastes. But how much better than the EU's Ode to Joy. This was a celebration of the uniqueness of nations – of their differences. And of mutual understanding of each other. How much better that recognition of "Vive la Difference" than some kind of artificial enforcement of conformity.

There is a lesson there for our post-Brexit relations with our European cousins.

4. Nationalism, Transnationalism or Supranationalism

"Where do we stand? We are not members of the European Defence Community, nor do we intend to be merged into a Federal European system. We feel we have a special relationship to both. We are with them, but not of them. We have our own Commonwealth and Empire..."

(Winston Churchill)

The EU itself faces a complex of threats, which could easily destabilise or even destroy it. The Euro remains unstable, growth historically very low. Some parts of the EU – Greece most obviously, but Portugal, perhaps Italy, Spain and Ireland – really cannot sustain the economic pace demanded by their stronger partners such as Germany. The likelihood of repeated Greece-type economic crises therefore seems high. More and more EU countries will face either central control by Germany, or terminal financial instability and economic depression.

Take Italy and her banking system, for example, which constantly teeters on the brink of an existential crisis. Italy is Europe's fourth biggest economy, yet one of its weakest. Public debt is at 135% of GDP; adult employment is lower than any other EU country except Greece, the economy is moribund, stifled by over-regulation, feeble productivity, stagnation and deflation. Italy's banks owe a staggering $400 Billion in bad debts, the equivalent of one fifth of the country's entire wealth. The likelihood of an imminent banking crisis of one sort or another seems very high.

So even were it not for Brexit, the consequences of which are still largely unknown, unquantifiable and unpredictable, the EU would be facing possibly existential challenges of its own making. Some would argue, indeed, that the ultimate destruction of the EU (and of similar historic attempts at supra-national dominance) was written into its very DNA. For the very act of trying to bind 743 million people of diverse cultures, languages, histories and above all economies into one straightjacket, is of itself a project doomed to failure. Empires (and the EU is most certainly a modern empire) cannot succeed and survive. Individualism and nationalism cannot be subsumed into the kind of collective will for the greatest good for the greatest number which you find in groups of human beings more readily defined by their nationhood.

Nations consist of people who are pretty much like one another, people of a more or less similar background, history, culture and language. The UK took 1000 years or so to be coherent enough to pull together wildly differing peoples. Angles,

26

Saxons, Normans, Jutes, Vikings, Celts and Brits. And that is without mentioning the diverse peoples from our old Empire and Commonwealth who are now proud to call our island shores their own. But collectively we have come to realise that 65 million people living on an island with a community of history, and interest is a reasonably logical unit of government.

By contrast to the relative hegemony of the UK, France, Spain (pace the Basques), and so on; and by contrast with the sole example of a nation being created from nought in a very short space of time in the United States of America, which forced diverse peoples spread over a sparsely-populated geography together into a broadly Anglo-Saxon liberal, free market democracy; by contrast with both, any historic attempt to pull together peoples with a diverse history, language or culture has always been doomed to failure.

The Romans tried it with a varying degree of success for 500 years or so. The British Empire was the greatest the world has ever seen using vast resources and brutal power to rule 500 million people across vast acreages of the globe. It lasted a maximum of 200 years. Soviet Communism tried it – for about 70 years; even Adolf Hitler thought it a good idea, only to be destroyed after a four-year war. Empires which try to pull together – or to govern by force – people with a diverse language or culture or history have a guaranteed failure gene at their heart.

It's always about a small group of super-intelligent elites who – largely for their own interests – propose an imperial solution. Precisely the same thing is happening in Europe today. What started off as a perfectly sensible trading arrangement amongst like-minded independent nation states has become a hideous quasi-empire as doomed to final failure as the others which went before it.

There were always some – Churchill and de Gaulle amongst them – who thought that the EU would prevent further European wars. Their generation was scarred by their personal experience in the Second World War, and many of them could very probably remember the First World War as well. That led them to argue that the EU, or Common Market, would prevent such a catastrophe happening again. I respect their view, but modestly suggest that their thinking on it all is a little woolly. Let us imagine that some mad dictator once again came to the fore – in Italy or Greece, Romania or Slovakia, for example. Do we really believe that their membership of the EU would somehow or another deter them from violence either internally or externally? Of course it would not. If the other circumstances are in place for there to be violent military

Winston Churchill with Charles De Gaulle.

conflicts, civil wars, invasions, or state on state warfare within the boundaries of the EU; the notion that the Brussels boffins would somehow or another prevent that happening is of course wholly laughable.

Not only that, but as Professor Sir Roger Scruton points out, *"those who believe that the division of Europe into nations has been the primary cause of European wars should remember the devastating wars of religion that national loyalties finally brought to an end."* He further points out that Nazism would not have been defeated without the national loyalty of the British people determined to defend their homeland.

The truth is that the EU has nothing to do with wars, and has no effective role in preventing them.

There are some bureaucratic enthusiasts who get quite carried away by the velocity of their own enthusiasm in every human institution – the Rugby Club always has some old bore more interested in the constitution of the club than in winning matches. Rules and Regulations, AGMs, SGMs, Committees, motions of no confidence, amalgamations, battles, reorganisations. These are the lifeblood of the constitutional bore. None of them helps the club score any goals.

Well there are plenty of exactly those sorts of people who end up in Brussels and Strasbourg. They love the European agenda not because it is any good to the peoples of Europe; they love it for its own sake. It's a form of self-perpetuating oligarchy.

The EU is a product of French distrust of Germany, and a 1000-year-old German determination to dominate the Continent. But does that Franco-German historic axis really justify the bureaucratic yoke which the EU is seeking to impose on the 750 million free people and nations of the Continent? I think not. Surely the only purpose in any governmental organisation must be the mutual benefit and betterment of the people it seeks to govern. The EU quite demonstrably does not have that aim at its heart.

The only genuine and justifiable purpose of the EU should be free trade amongst its member states. That could be very easily achieved by mutual or bilateral agreements to abolish trade barriers.

The Europhile truism which lies behind much of the Euro superstate project can be summarised (without I hope any exaggeration or parody) as follows.

'We are being left behind by the emerging economic superpowers. China and the whole Far East on one extreme, and the Americas on the other. How can small nation states – some of us with as few as 10/15 million inhabitants – hope to compete with superpowers like that? We need to get together as one great amalgam economically if we are to stand an outside chance of keeping up with them.'

A vast infrastructure of equally spurious arguments – including, for example, the wholly illogical conclusion that we need a European Foreign Service and a European army to look after our interests – follows from that pretty tenuous premise. It's a complex yet easily refuted premise. The proposal that 'The Far East' or 'The Americas' or even the BRIC Nations form single coherent economic and trading groupings against which we need to collude to compete, is of course absurd.

Tell the Japanese that they are part of China's trading ambit and that therefore they need a single currency, convergence of economies, joint infrastructure development, an internal market, far less a joint government, banking system, foreign policy or army, and you would expose yourself at very least to ridicule. Try telling the Americans or even the Canadians that their continuation as a super-power depends on similar cooperation with Mexico or even with Brazil. Try telling India that 'The Great Game' is now ancient history, and economic alliance with China is the only way forward. Yet it is arguments of this sort which have for years been advanced as the most fundamental of all justifications for the EU.

What nonsense it is. Japan is great on her own, despite her small island geography and her population of 128 million, and despite the stagnation of her economy over many years. India and Brazil are pulling themselves up by their bootstraps, and will without doubt be important economies in the Twenty-First Century. But that is not because of any kind of intergovernmental infrastructure. India is not entering into some kind of alliance with Bhutan, Nepal, Bangladesh and Pakistan. Brazil would no more have a United States of Latin America including Bolivia, Ecuador and Argentina than we should look forward to a United States of Europe with Turkey, Finland, Lithuania and Poland.

These are artificial constructs; castles in the air created by the European chattering classes on a wet Wednesday afternoon. And they take no account of economic or political or human realities of life. The EU is also unique in being a truly supranational organisation, a body which purports to be 'above' its member nation states. That of course is in sharp contrast to 'multi-national' as opposed to supra-national organisations such as the UN, NATO, EFTA, ASEAN, the Arab League and so on. They are voluntary co-operations amongst free and independent nation states who may or may not take part fully or partially. The EU is a unique experiment attempting to bind Nation States together with an irreversible supranational ratchet effect. The seeds of its ultimate failure were by that means sewn into its very fabric.

The fact of the matter is that technological advances make international trading blocs like the European Union outdated. We no longer need supra-governments to monitor and handle our trading. Human beings can buy and sell things to each other across the globe in a matter of seconds. We just don't need the supposed economic muscle of the EU to allow it to occur.

The EU and its infrastructure and bureaucracy is to world trade as the Royal Mail is to communication and as the corner shop is to internet shopping. We all love the Royal Mail, and it has a huge role to play in ensuring a universal obligation to deliver letters to every address in the UK, however remote. But there can be no doubt about it – its survival is seriously challenged by emails and the internet short-cutting laborious and slow communication by post. Internet shopping offers similar challenges to our high street shops.

International trade doesn't need to be controlled by an unelected bunch of bureaucrats in Brussels constructing ever-more complex restrictions and exclusivities. The World Trade Organisation is vastly more important. Clearing away constraints and restrictions on trade; liberalising the buying and selling of goods across the globe is so very much more important than small-minded small market Europeanism.

Trade outside the EU under WTO terms would be a great deal less catastrophic than some ardent 'Remainers' would have you believe. The UK's visible trade deficit with the EU was £89 billion in 2015, (i.e. we imported £89 billion more from the EU than we exported to them.) The deficit with Germany alone was £31 billion; with Holland £15 billion, Belgium-Luxembourg £10 billion; with Italy £7 billion, France £6 billion and Spain £5 billion. The notion that we might 'stop trading' with them is frankly ludicrous. But if in some fairy-land that were to happen, it would damage each of those countries far more than it would damage the UK.

Over the period 2005-2015, UK exports expanded by 50%. Yet the growth to EU countries was only 25%, a 75% growth to non-EU countries trading under WTO terms. Exports to South Korea grew by over 130%; to Turkey by 80%, to South Africa by 25%. Exports to China (with whom there is no preferential trading deal) grew in the same period by 350%. The US remains our single biggest export market. Even exports to Russia grew by nearly 25%. (Figures from Ruth Lea.)

So quite plainly trade with non-EU countries under WTO rules thrives without any kind of preferential trade agreements. In the absence of any other agreement with the EU, there is really very little reason to presume that trade with an EU country would be not equally buoyant under WTO.

The fact is that technology has instantly shrunk the globe. It used to take us weeks to send a letter to India, months to receive back the goods we wanted to buy. Nowadays we are truly one world, one marketplace. The EU is looking tired and outdated as an economic and trading necessity.

So supra-national organisations like the EU may be amusing playthings for the super-bureaucrats whose bright brains have had enough of bridge and prize crosswords, and seek to apply them to world affairs. But the truth of the matter is that all of history tells us that any such construct has the opposite effect to that sought. Any artificially created attempt to tell the birds of one particular feather that they must flock together with birds of a wholly different feather is doomed to fail.

The UK works as a construct because we are all of one culture and history (after 1000 years or more of creating it.) That means that the richer bits are more or less content to subsidise the poorer bits, and as a general rule we rub along together pretty well. Scottish and Welsh nationalists will ultimately fail in their sentimental attempts to undo the work of 400 years (since the Union of the Crowns in 1603 and the Union of the Parliaments in 1707) for the very simple reason that Britain – like France, Germany, Spain and Holland – represents a sensible and publicly understandable unit of government. The Roman Empire, the British Empire, and the EU by clear contrast, however, are not.

World peace, prosperity, an end to hunger and poverty will be achieved not by supra-national attempts to force people to do what they would really rather not be doing. Instead it will be accomplished by harnessing their natural ambitions and prejudices and self-interest to recognise that doing things together is a great deal better in the long run than doing them separately, or even worse in opposition to one another.

So much was recognised by Locke, Hume and the rest who lauded a Social Contract, in which people agree to abide by laws and help a mutual economy because they realise that despite government's short-term irritations and inconveniences, it is overall and in the longer term in their own personal interests. These are the instincts which we must harness and expand if we are to leave the world a better place than it was when we found it. And our energies would be much better used trying to do so than in trying to create artificial and ultimately doomed to failure supra-national constructs like the EU.

Empires try to bind together people who are unlike one another. For that reason – as the EU may now be discovering – they cannot succeed. The seeds of its own destruction were written into the 'ever-closer union' language of the Treaty of Rome itself.

So the EU is not for us. Like Groucho Marx: *'{We} wouldn't want to join a club that would have {us}'*. But if the EU's not for us, then what is?

5. Vive La Spirite Olympique

"Swifter, Higher, Stronger." (Pierre de Coubertin)

If we are to know what we are for in the world; if we are to stand any chance of laying out some kind of grand vision of our future; if we are to puzzle over which road to take at this great historic cross roads, we must start from some notion of who we are. What are our national characteristics? What is it that motivates us?

Perhaps a glance at Danny Boyle's mildly eccentric opening pageant for the London Olympics in 2012 may give us a few sideways glimpses of our national characteristics, or at least of how we view ourselves, which may of course be different?

There was a touch of most things British in it – from yokels with straws in their mouths and the peace of the eighteenth century rural landscape through a cigar chomping Isambard Kingdom Brunel supervising the rolling up of the green carpet and its replacement with smoke and grime and muck and brass. There was Mr Bean helping the LSO with the theme tune from *Chariots of Fire*; there was the tribute to that great British institution, the National Health Service, followed by a wholly mystifying parable of a lost mobile phone and the love affair surrounding its reunion with its rightful owner, which allowed a focus on the British inventor of the World Wide Web, Sir Tim Berners-Lee. There was a passing reference to Churchill with his Parliament Square statue coming to life, a glimpse of a Guards Band, a view of the Mother of Parliaments from the London Eye.

The whole thing culminated in fireworks second to none, the arrival of the Olympic flame in a speed boat apparently piloted up the Thames by David Beckham; and a genuinely brilliant piece of engineering bringing a myriad Olympic flames together into a huge cauldron. It was magnificent, very British, a bit dotty, and completely incomprehensible to most people, especially foreigners, to whom it must have seemed rather a weird way of advertising all that is great about one's country.

Do you remember that great moment at the start of it all when James Bond was shown in to the Drawing Room at Buckingham Palace by a tailcoated footman? The Queen was writing at her desk. 'It can't be,' we all thought. But then she turned around with a cool "Good evening, Mr Bond." It IS her we thrilled, as she was escorted to the waiting helicopter and parachuted in to the stadium. What a brilliant idea; what superb choreography. Really how very British in every way.

Yet what happened as HM arrived at her seat in the Royal Box? *"Et maintenant, Mesdames et Messieurs, je suis tres heureux a introduire Sa Majeste et Duc d'Edimbourg. Bienvenue a Londres 2012."* Or some such. "A Frenchman welcoming the Queen to the London Olympics," we all thought to ourselves. "What on earth is going on

London 2012, Olympic opening ceremony.

A miniature version of London landmarks at the 2012 Olympic closing ceremony.

33

here? Probably some new outrage from the ghastly European Union." Even those of us who realised that this was all to do with Olympic protocol deriving from Baron Pierre de Coubertin, the founder of the modern Olympics, were to a greater or lesser degree discomfited. It's not that we are Xenophobic or anti-French. It's just that we are very much British.

Nationalism is all about hating other peoples' countries (as evidenced by the Scottish Nationalists); patriotism is about loving one's own country. And the 2012 and 2016 Olympics were shining examples of true British patriotism. For behind it all – running through its weft and weave – was an almost unspoken undercurrent that Britain is Great, and that we Britons have a quiet assurance that that is the case.

There was a firmly patriotic flavour to the competitions themselves as well, both in 2012, and even more so in 2016. How is it that little Britain – only 65 million people and most of us overfed couch potatoes like me – could come second in the medals league tables in 2016, behind only the American giants with their huge populations and sports spending and determination, and beating China into a humiliating third place? 193 nations took part in the 2016 Games. Of them only 54 won gold medals, only 3 having won more than twenty. There is little direct correlation between the league table of medals won and any balance of power, wealth or influence in the world. Hungary, for example, was twelfth in the hierarchy, Cuba performed better than Canada who only narrowly beat Uzbekistan (13 medals) and Kazakhstan (17 including 3 golds) and India managed only 1 silver and 1 bronze.

Nor is it solely about money invested in sport. Despite the huge contribution from Sir John Major's Lottery which must take a lot of the credit, our 'pounds invested per medal achieved' ratio is very likely to be one of the lowest. I suspect that Jamaica must be pretty good too. Someone should do the statistical analysis.

So it was not sheer numbers of the populace which drove our medals success in the London Olympics. It was not state funding; and it was not about state education in the way that it is in Russia or America either.

So what was it? Well I'll tell you what I think it was about. And it's a curiously un-British thing to say. It was about patriotism. We Brits don't like to talk about it, and we are shy about showing it. The Americans love clapping their hands to their left breast and standing to attention every time they see the Stars and Stripes or hear *God Bless America*. We are much more reticent, more self-deprecating about it. But underneath our shy exterior we are actually immensely patriotic. Our national reticence, our inherent modesty, deserts us on certain occasions. Great royal events, great state occasions, great sporting events.

We love our country and its little ways. We love it like it is and don't want it to change. We love its little eccentricities, and won't hear a word said against it. Betjeman was not being entirely ironic when he considered what our nation stands for:

Books from Boots and country lanes; Free Speech, free passes, class distinction, Democracy and proper drains.

Ours is a funny little island race. We are the product of thousands of years of turbulent history. We are a mixture of peoples and traditions. We are an ancient, monarchical, slightly anarchistic, individualistic, entrepreneurial, mildly bonkers, mainly polite and decent bunch of islanders. We match the weather – not perfect but it does a good job by and large.

We know that there is nothing in the world to beat the NHS. We are proud of our sporting excellence. We like the eccentricities of our great constitution, and especially our monarchy. We have a sneaking suspicion that our execrable cooking is nonetheless good for us, and that our horrible weather keeps us healthy and the countryside green. We love the Bobby on the beat, the comfortable negativity of BBC Radio 4's *Today* Programme and the obscure braininess of *University Challenge*. It's about *The Archers*, the pre-Raphaelites and Elgar; the Chartists, Tolpuddle Martyrs and Suffragettes, about self-deprecating irony. It's about Del Boy, Basil Fawlty and Hyacinth Bucket, about Eddie the Eagle, and a slight embarrassment at winning the 1966 World Cup.

Britain is where we know the form, where decency prevails; where the trains are dirty and slow; where vicars ride on bicycles, and where we like to drink warm brown bitter beer and eat fish and chips. As Elizabeth Aston said: "England is a place of kings and queens; of Runnymede and Shakespeare's London; of hansom cabs and Sherlock Homes and Dr Watson rattling off into the fog with cries of 'The Games afoot', of civil wars… and spotted pigs and Churchill and his country standing alone against the might of Nazi Germany."

Of course we like to moan and groan. The weather is our favourite grumble, despite a steadfast scepticism about climate change. The cricket is next, and especially the government, no matter who may be in power. We are genuinely concerned about the way the nation is going at any one moment. There's always a grumpy old git at one corner of the bar ready to tell you that the country is 'going to hell in a handcart.' It's not usually about health and education which, oddly enough, we by and large believe to be excellent. Nor, usually, is it about jobs and the economy. It's about law and order, immigration, Europe, Health and Safety, ministerial incompetence. It's about our great armed services and how much they are let down both by government and by senior officers; and overall it's about how 'it wasn't like this in my young day.'

It was ever thus. I take great comfort from the Venerable Bede, who, writing around 600AD decries the way that young people these days wear their hair far too long, and drink alcohol in excess!

Yet behind our self-deprecation and moaning (which stands in such stark contrast to, for example, the Americans who habitually go to the opposite extreme to tell you how wonderful their country is and everything in it), the fact of the matter is that in our heart of hearts we still believe that Britain is Great, nay the Greatest.

George Orwell tried to sum it all up in a series of war-time articles (although he personally dismissed them at the time as being 'propaganda for the British Council.') In 'England Your England', 'The English People', and 'My Country Right or Left', he tried to capture the qualities of Englishness as he perceived them in the 1940s. His perceptions have stuck with us ever since.

The English, Orwell said *"were inefficient but with sound instincts"*, chief amongst which were *"gentleness"* and *"respect for constitutionalism and legality."* We had an intense sensitivity to class. *"I was born into what you might call the lower-upper-middle class."* Our patriotism was thick headed – *"the bulldog is an animal noted for its obstinacy, ugliness and stupidity"*– and proudly insular. *"Nearly every Englishman of working-class origin considers it effeminate to pronounce a foreign word correctly."* One of his most famous descriptions – "old maids biking to Holy Communion" – was fifty years later, perhaps unconsciously, quoted by Sir John Major in a Party Conference speech.

The British "addiction to hobbies and spare-time occupations, the privateness of English life…All the culture that is most truly native, centres around things which even when they are communal are not official – the pub, the football match, the back garden, the fireside and 'a nice cup of tea'."

Orwell's patriotism was rooted in enduring values and attitudes. Key to the English character was anti-militarism. The goose-step *"is not used here, because the people in the street would laugh."* We celebrate defeats and retreats, like Corunna, Gallipoli and Dunkirk. *"The most stirring battle-poem in English is about a brigade of cavalry which charged in the wrong direction."*

So that is who we are. A little island nation defined by many national peculiarities; a maritime nation with sea links to the wider world, proudly independent of Europe, a product of empire and history.

Robert Winder's book *The Last Wolf: The Hidden Springs of Englishness* gives another sideways thought about Englishness. *"What makes and forms a people,"* says Winder, *"is the one thing they all share: the place itself. If there is an 'Englishness' it is formed from the nature, literally, of England. If we really want to look for our national identity, the real place to look was in the natural heritage of hills, valleys, rivers, stones and mists – the raw materials that had, over time, moulded the way we were. Landscape and history – the past and the elemental backdrop – were the only things we could truly claim as our own. Just as some plants thrive in sand and others in clay, so a natural character is fed by nutrients it cannot alter."*

The novelist, Lawrence Durrell made the same case, perhaps more provocatively: *"I believe that you could exterminate the French at a blow and resettle the land with Tartars, and within two generations discover that the national characteristics were back at the norm – the relentless metaphysical curiosity, the tenderness for good living and the passionate individualism."* Durrell goes on to suggest that *"a Cypriot who settled in*

London would in time become English, simply because human customs owe as much to local environment as to trees and flowers."

American patriotism is a caricature of itself. Ours is far more genuine. We love the fact that we used to have pounds, shillings and pence in defiance of any possible logic, and that we still have the pound in defiance of the mighty euro. We stick resolutely to driving on the left-hand side of the road and to measuring distances in miles, and to pints of bitter beer.

Yet our concept of ourselves is not just about vicars on bicycles and soggy cabbage. We turn out in our droves for great events like the funerals of Princess Diana and the Queen Mother; the Royal Wedding, and the Diamond Jubilee Celebrations. We drape ourselves in national flags at football matches round the world; our high streets are bedecked with nationalistic bunting. The spirit of the people of Wootton Bassett in my constituency caught the imagination of the whole country and of the world when they turned out five deep in all weathers on 167 occasions to mark the 'Repatriation' of 345 soldiers' bodies from Iraq and Afghanistan. The renaming of the town 'Royal Wootton Bassett' is well deserved. We are truly patriotic in a very real sense. We are Great Britain and we love being it.

With the Royal Wootton Bassett flag on the South Pole, 2016.

That spirit of national pride was in evidence in spades at the Olympics. It's almost as if we need some great national event to take ourselves out from behind our modesty and shyness and collectively to fly the flag. Our teams and competitors could feel it in a very real way. The winners could not wait to grasp the first Union flag which came to hand and bedeck themselves in it. There was something of "It's not Ennis...It's not Nick Skelton... It's the British team. It's Great Britain."

What cannot be gainsaid is that whatever our defining characteristics, or even our self-defining ones, we are different to the French. France is only 22 miles away across the Channel, but it's a crucial 22 miles. 22 miles separating two vastly different, contrasting and competing cultures.

22 miles away is a foreign land where they speak a peculiar lingo; where they eat garlic in excess, and are a little unkeen on baths. They are frogs; we are spanking Rosbifs. They are Roman Catholics; since Henry Vlll's divorce, we are Protestants (although curiously the more extreme Calvinist Protestants amongst us – the Scots – are much closer to our Gallic cousins.) We espouse R. H. Tawney's Protestant Work Ethic. They are idle, romantic, charming and artistic. We are dull, hardworking and pragmatic. They make love twice a day; we do it on Anniversaries and occasionally on a Saturday after the football. They eat *Pate de Foie Gras*; we eat rump steaks. Never can there have been such a perceived cultural divide over a 22-mile waterway than that between Dover and Calais.

6. The Englishman's Moat

"We have the character of an island nation: independent, forthright, passionate in defence of our sovereignty. We can no more change this British sensibility than we can drain the English Channel."
(David Cameron – if only he had stuck by it!)

Our curiously eccentric, modest, often hidden, patriotism has for centuries defined the very nature of our relationship with the rest of the world. How we view ourselves is central to how we view other people. Are we at one with them? Are they our brothers and sisters? Do we look down on them? Seek to rule or improve them? Or do we view them with suspicion and derision? Do we respect them, or do we fear them?

We may start to get some feel for that from the history, and changes, in one iconic and essential strip of water – the English Channel, *La Manche*, the Englishman's Moat. It separates us from the rest of the world, but also in a curious way connects us to it. Numerous wars have been fought across it; it has acted as the last bastion of our defence and of the defence of civilisation and democracy on many occasions. Yet it is also our route to the wider world through our shipping and trading instincts and history. There is no more significant geographic feature to our nation than the Channel. It both separates us from the Continent of Europe and is our link to it.

"The Channel is that silver strip of sea which severs merry England from the tardy realms of Europe." (Unattributed)

Shakespeare knew it too:-

"This Royal throne of kings, this sceptred isle,
This earth of majesty, this seat of Mars,
This other Eden, demi-paradise,
This fortress built by Nature for herself
Against infection and the hand of war,
This happy breed of men, this little world,
This precious stone set in the silver sea,
Which serves it in the office of a wall
Or as a moat defensive to a house,
Against the envy of less happier lands –
This blessed plot, this earth, this Realm, this England."
(Shakespeare, *Richard II*)

"Britannia needs no bulwarks
No towers along the steep;
Her march is o'er the mountain wave
Her home is on the deep."
(Thomas Campbell, *Ye Mariners of England.*)

"Abroad, it is said, begins at Calais." (Anon.)

The Channel runs 350 miles from the Straits of Dover to a line joining the Scilly Isles with the isle of Ushant. It varies in width from 150 miles at its widest (Britanny to Dorset) to 20.6 miles in the Strait of Dover. It covers an area of 29,000 square miles, with an average depth of 270 feet ranging up to 571 feet at a remarkable narrow trough north of the Channel Islands called Hurd's Deep. It is of geologically recent origin, having been dry land for most of the Pleistocene period. Before the end of the most recent Ice Age, about 1,000,000 years ago, Britain and Ireland were linked to mainland Europe by a landbridge called the Weald-Artois Anticline. It was that Anticline breaking between 450,000 and 180,000 years ago which caused two catastrophic glacial lake outbursts. There was apparently a huge glacial lake in the Doggerlands, an area now buried by the North Sea, but whose name is gleefully commemorated in the Shipping Forecast. Presumably as a result of some kind of global warming, the ice barrier containing it broke, and the resulting flooding caused the English Channel. The flood would have lasted for many months, apparently releasing as much as one million cubic metres of water per second. That massive flow of water scoured a channel through an expanse of low-lying tundra, right down to the underlying chalk bedrock. Scientists say that the scour marks are still clearly visible beneath the English Channel.

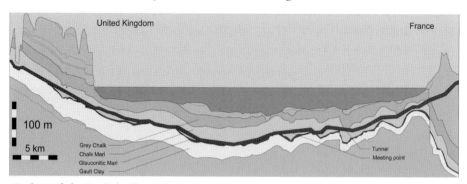

Geology of the English Channel.

The English Channel is not, in fact, wholly English, since our territorial waters extend only 12 miles from the coast. So, it could equally justifiably be called the French Channel, or perhaps the Belgian one. Yet the name 'The English Channel' has been widely used by English-speaking peoples at least since the eighteenth century. The British Channel or British Sea seems to have been more common before that since perhaps Ptolemy called it Oceanicus Britannicus in the second century. The Anglo Saxons called it the South Sea (as opposed to the North Sea which of course continues until today). The word Channel is first recorded in English in the thirteenth century, being derived from the French word Canal.

It was an Italian map of about 1450 which first used the expression 'Canalites Angliae.' The French name, *'La Manche'* has been in use since the seventeenth century, and is commonly thought to derive from the French word for a sleeve. But there is also a Celtic word, which is still used in the North of Scotland, where the waters between Orkney and the mainland is called 'The Minch.' The Breton language also being of Celtic origin, that would seem to me to be the most likely derivation.

The existence of the Channel apparently delayed the repopulation of Britain by 100,000 years, until our Continental neighbours learned to use a boat. Remnants of a Mesolithic (10,000-5000 BC) boatyard have been found in the Isle of Wight. Wheat was traded across the Channel about 8000 years ago, and the Ferriby boats, Hanson log boats and the later Bronze Age Dover boat could carry substantial cargo across the Channel.

That may be an early indication of the Channel's dual role in the thousands of years since. It is both an easy entry for seafaring peoples and a barrier to unwelcome invasion. The Spanish Armada, Napoleon, the Nazis were all defeated by the Channel, although the Romans (Julius Caesar in 55 then 54 BC although it took another ten years before Britain was fully a part of the Roman Empire under Aulus Plautius) and the Normans, of course, were not. In the power vacuum left by the retreating Romans, waves of Germanic Angles, Saxons and Jutes came across the North Sea, and no doubt the English Channel as well, displacing the native Celtic populations. The Vikings followed them from the attack on Lindisfarne in 753 AD for 250 years after which the Danes, Norwegians and Swedes dominated the North Sea. The Anglo- Saxon Chronicle has it that they started to settle in Britain in 851 and kept doing so until about 1050. And of course their very name, the Normans, reminds us of William the Conqueror's Norse ancestry.

Leaving warfare on one side, the Channel also facilitated great alliances. The Norman control of both England and Normandy ran from 1066 to 1204, when King John lost it to Philip II, although we kept control of the Channel Islands until modern times. The Angevin Empire from 1135 to 1217 easily spanned the Channel, and Henry II regained Normandy in 1259. His descendants fought to hold it until Tudor times, Calais, of course, being inscribed on Bloody Mary's heart. ("When I am dead and opened, you shall find Calais lying in my heart.") It was not until 1801 that the British surrendered their claims to mainland Normandy and other French possessions, and to this day, the Monarch is known as 'The Duke of Normandy' when she is in the Channel Islands. The Loyal Toast in Jersey is to *"La Reine, Notre Duc."*

From Tudor times onwards, the Channel became not so much a trading waterway as a means of preventing unwanted invasions. Notable naval battles in the Channel include the defeat of the Spanish Armada, the Battle of the Downs (1639), the Battle of Goodwin Sands and the Battle of Portland (1652) the Battle of La Hougue (1692) and the engagement between USS *Kearsarge* and CSS *Alabama* in 1864.

The Channel facilitated the greatest sea invasion of all time – the Normandy Landings in 1944. A 50-mile stretch of the Normandy coast, divided into the famous five beaches (Utah, Omaha, Gold, Juno and Sword) saw a total of 153,000 troops going ashore from 7000 vessels, protected and assisted by 3000 aircraft and gliders. There was a total of 425,000 casualties more or less evenly split between the allies and the Germans. Never had the world seen such a massive assault, and never will it again.

A convoy of Landing Craft Infantry sails across the English Channel toward the Normandy Invasion beaches on D-Day, 6 June 1944.

It is said, perhaps apocryphally, that if you Google "Famous French Naval Victories," the answer comes back "No Match Found." The two great English victories over the French – at Waterloo and Trafalgar – are commemorated by two vast murals in the Royal Gallery of the House of Lords. They were covered over by brown paper when de Gaulle addressed both Houses there in 1946. There were no similar sensibilities observed when President Sarkozy repeated the experience in 2008, as a result of which neither he nor the Speaker could understand our school-boy tittering when Michael Martin referred to 'this great Palace and the wonderful works of art in it.'

The growth in the Royal Navy to be the most powerful in the world is due in no small part to the need to defend the English Channel against invasion. The exceptional strategic importance of the Channel was firmly recognised during the Spanish Wars of the sixteenth and seventeenth centuries, the French Wars in the eighteenth and nineteenth and of course the German Wars of the twentieth century. The First Sea Lord in the First World War, Admiral Lord Fisher, famously opined that the five keys to the world were Singapore, the Cape of Good Hope, Alexandria, Gibraltar and Dover. The Royal Navy of course firmly dominated all five at the time.

It was the Royal Navy's pre-eminence which forced the Germans to start to develop under-sea capability and invent the submarine, which in the end became a far greater threat to Britain than the surface fleet. The early part of the First World War, and indeed arguably the reason for it becoming bogged down in the awful war of attrition in the trenches, was a race to the Channel ports. Both the Kaiser and the Brits knew that control of the Channel ports could well be absolutely decisive in the war. At the outset of the war, an attempt was made to prevent German submarines from entering the English Channel by minefields and eventually by a 20-mile stretch of light steel netting called the Dover Barage. Both were being rendered useless by 1917, when the Germans restarted submarine warfare leading to the Passchendaele attempt to capture the German submarine bases on the Belgian coast. And in 1918, the famous Zeebrugge raid was against the U-Boat bases.

As one of the narrowest, but most iconic, of all waterways, the Channel has been the target of numerous famous crossings. In March 1816, the French paddle steamer *Elise* was the first to cross the Channel. The paddle steamer *Rob Roy* was the first passenger ferry in 1821, Folkestone/Boulogne opening in 1843. 1959 saw the first hovercraft; 1974 the first coracle; 1997 the first solar-powered crossing. Others have crossed by car (BBC's *Top Gear*), by waterski, by sea scooter. The first hot air balloon crossing was in 1785 (Jean Pierre Francois Blanchard and American John Jeffries).

It was in 25 July 1909 that Louis Bleriot successfully made the first Channel crossing by aeroplane, which signalled the end of the Channel as a barrier-moat for England against foreign enemies. That in a sense culminated in the Battle of Britain in 1940. The sport of swimming across the Channel was started by Captain Matthew Webb on 24/25 August, 1875 when he was the first to cross (in a time of 21 hours and 45 minutes.) As he is reported to have said, "Nothing great is easy" (perhaps a metaphor for Brexit?). The fastest crossing was by the Australian Trent Grimsey on 8 September 2012 in 6 hours and 55 minutes. By the end of 2005, 811 people had completed 1185 verified crossings; there had been 16 two-way crossings, and three three-way crossings (two by men and one by a woman.)

Until recently, the appalling squalor of the "Jungle" camp at Calais, full of mainly Middle Eastern and North African young men willing to do anything to come to these shores was somehow symbolic of the divide between us and our French cousins and neighbours. The building of the Tunnel was feared by some at the time to mean an end to our Sovereignty.

Many Xenophobes and Little Englanders would have echoed the remarks of Theodore Nook in 1825 in John Bull:

"A tunnel underneath the sea from Calais straight to Dover, Sir. The squeamish folks may cross by land from shore to shore. With sluices made to drown the French, if e'er they would come over, Sir, has long been talked of, till at length is thought a monstrous bore."

Our determined defence against unwelcome immigrants at its other end may in fact symbolise the opposite.

The English Channel is the World's busiest waterway with about 500 ships transiting it every day. To prevent accidents, which were frequent in the past, the London-based International Maritime Organisation mandated in the Dover Traffic Separation system that ships going north use the French side, with those traveling south using the English side. The safe navigation of this often treacherous strip of water is due at least in part to the ministrations of a little-known organisation based at Tower Hill in London, and controlling and maintaining lighthouses, light vessels, maritime training and a host of related activities. It is a Henry Vlll foundation called Trinity House, one of whose 'Younger Brothers' I am proud to have been appointed – the Labour MP Jim FitzPatrick and I being the first ever Members of Parliament to be so honoured.

It is a much over-used word, but there is something truly iconic about this great waterway. It is as significant to us as the St Lawrence is to Canada, the Hudson to New York, the Amazon to Brazil or the Nile to Egypt. In a very real way it truly defines our nationality and our nation's history.

We are an island nation, a nation of seafarers and traders, defined by the seas which surround us, most particularly by the Channel. We do not consider ourselves to be 'European.' We are 'British' or 'English' or 'Wiltshiremen.' We do not recognise the EU flag, nor sing their anthem. We could not name the President of the European Union, nor do we know the difference between the European Parliament, the Council of Ministers, the European Commission, nor indeed that wholly unrelated organisation, the Council of Europe (which numbers amongst its members, the Russians). We are not aware that the European Court of Human Rights is a great deal older than the European Union, and is a wholly different organisation to the European Court of Justice.

We Brits pay little attention to these matters. We are just not interested; we have no identity with them. That attitude of mind – which is at its heart why we voted to leave – is wholly different to that of our Continental neighbours, who truly see themselves as Europeans. And it is the English Channel which has created that feeling of difference, of distance from the Continent of Europe.

Cynics sneer at 'Little Englanders.' But the truth is that that really is what we are, or certainly much more so than 'Large Europeaners.'

7. Britain in the World

"If you lead a country like Britain, a strong country, a country which has taken a lead in world affairs in good times and in bad, a country that is always reliable, then you have to have a touch of iron about you."

(Margaret Thatcher)

So if it's not to be the EU, then what is it? Where do we fit in the world? Britain was 'Great' once (although we were not in fact 'great' at the time that Ptolemy first coined the expression to differentiate us from 'Lesser Britain' - the Island of Ireland.) Of that there can be no doubt. The empire, the Industrial Revolution, Elizabeths I and II, the Mother of Parliaments and our 1000-year-old constitution which is the stable envy of unstable nations everywhere; the first proper Navy, the best and greatest armies in the world; our inventions – TV and broadcasting, Penicillin, Concorde, the Worldwide Web; our language that is at last becoming the *'lingua franca'* of the entire world. Can there ever have been a 'greater' nation? 'Certainly not' most reasonable people would probably agree.

Yet if we asked the very same people (whether British or from overseas) the question "Is Britain Great today", there would without doubt be a bit of shuffling of the feet, eyes downcast, caveats, mumbling and uncertainty. That may partly be our British character. Such an opinion poll (if they had then existed) conducted at the height of our 'Greatness' – let's say around 1880 – might well have met with a similar degree of uncertainty and modesty which is the first of our identifiable national characteristics.

We are even less certain about our role in the world. That may have been clear at the height of empire, or perhaps when we faced real and immediate threats – the two World Wars, the Argentinian invasion of the Falklands, the Iraqi invasion of Kuwait. Our role at those times was clear. By contrast, most people today would ask "What were we really doing in Iraq in 2003, and in Hellmand Province, Afghanistan through until 2014?" "Were the bodies of our brave young soldiers carried down Royal Wootton Bassett High Street really worth it? And should we really be bombing Daesh in Iraq and Syria today?" Questions like that would find a great deal less unanimity.

But let's then ask the question "Can Britain be Great again in the future – at home or abroad?" I think most Brits at least would be pretty confident in their answer. "Of course we can." We are a great nation, the fourth richest in the world, the land of freedom and democracy; the land of business and prosperity, of fine farmlands and rich mineral wealth; the land where decency and good management are taught in our great schools and universities. Our second place in the 2016

Olympic medals table is symbolic of our greatness in so many other areas. We can truly be a 'Top Nation' (in the memorable words of that best of all books of history, Sellars and Yeatman's 1066 And All That) if we put our minds to it. Of course Britain can be Great again. Of course we can prove the conclusion to Sellars and Yeatman's final chapter entitled 'A Bad Thing' to be wrong. (You will remember that they concluded that *"America was thus clearly top nation and history came to a ."*) But did it? And what role can little Britain have in restarting it?

In other words, the Question before the House (as we MPs would say) is: what is Britain really for? Are we a great nation? Do we have a real role to play in the wider world? Or are we historically great, but now consigned to the sidelines of history? Do we have the military, diplomatic and economic resources to be a truly great force for good in the world? Does our imperial past, or even our self-interested present give us a moral or actual obligation to 'punch above our weight' in Global matters? Are we right in thinking that we have a great deal to offer the wider world and all of the challenges it currently faces?

If we are to face the future – the future of disturbances in the Middle East and Asia Minor, the future of mass migrations of homeless people, of terrorism, of uncertainty about the post-Brexit European Union, of the generational battle between Sunni and Shia (Saudi Arabia vs Iran and through proxy wars in Yemen and Syria), of the US and China eyeing each other's greatness across the Pacific, of Russia's new-found confidence and expansionism; if we are to face all of that we must truly make a grand strategic plan as to what role we are to have in it all, and what we must do for the best interests of the people of Britain.

The government has a body who are supposed to do that kind of thing, called the National Security Council. But their five-yearly publication of the National Security Strategy is a pretty poor little rag of a document hovering between the obvious and the banal. It is certainly not truly strategic. The Parliamentary Committee which monitors the NSS has, over the seven years of its existence, been unremittingly critical of it, pointing to its less than strategic approach, its failure to address any areas of problem, no matter how high profile, or to delineate lessons learned from them. Similar criticisms are levelled at the National Security Committee which is supposed to convert the NSS into action.

The military do have a department – the Development Concepts and Doctrine Centre – whose job it is to think the unthinkable; to project forward twenty or thirty years what warfare will be like in the future; and to try to make us ready for whatever may come our way. Their "Global Strategic Trends" which stretches its critical eye out to 2045, is a magnificent effort to determine which direction the world is going in, and therefore what kind of warfare may be most likely in the future. From it comes their "Future Operating Environment 2035" and then their "Future Force Concept 2035."

All together it amounts to a serious attempt to analyse global trends, and predict the resulting military mix. It is useful background information for the now regular Strategic Defence and Security Reviews. But the harsh reality is that all of that work is thereafter largely ignored by the Treasury who blithely cut our military and diplomatic budgets whenever they can without undue political embarrassment, cheerfully unaware, or uninterested, in our long term strategic goals and positioning in the world.

The government conduct a five-yearly Strategic Defence and Security Review. But again, if the military is not funded properly, there is little point in the SDSR as it is known. And at all events, SDSR lacks any real grand vision as to what we are truly about in the world. The SDSR in 2010, for example, was blissfully unaware of the Arab Spring, it saw no state on state risk, not even from Russia, which it listed as a good friend if not ally. More alarmingly still it failed to foresee our withdrawal from Afghanistan, and made no mention of ISIS or Islamic Fundamentalist Jihadi warfare. The 2015 SDSR had caught up a bit. But like all such documents it tends to 'fight the last war.' There is, for example, no mention of the North Atlantic or Arctic, which many experts predict will be an increasingly dangerous area in the future.

So what is our role in the world post-Brexit? Are we a force for good on our own, through NATO, perhaps still in partnership with the EU? Is our national place as a member of successive coalitions of the willing as we were in Iraq and Afghanistan? Do we agree with the American NeoCons that Western Democracy, with its free liberal economies is just so demonstrably a 'good thing' that we are legally and morally justified in seeking to impose our accepted wisdoms on countries so unfortunate as not to have realised it around the world?

That, after all, was pretty much the thinking behind the British Empire until the 1960s or so. Fifty years ago, we believed that we had a God-given right and obligation to impose our system of capitalism and government – as well, of course, of religion – on the rest of the unfortunate world. As Violet Bonham Carter said in her biography of Churchill : -

"The world of 1906...was a stable and a civilized world in which the greatness and authority of Britain and her Empire seemed unassailable and invulnerably secure. In spite of our reverses in the Boer War it was assumed unquestioningly that we should always emerge 'victorious, happy and glorious' from any conflict. There were no doubts about the permanence of our 'dominion over palm and pine', or of our title to it. Powerful, prosperous, peace-loving, with the seas all round us and the Royal Navy on the seas, the social, economic, international order seemed to our unseeing eyes as firmly fixed on earth as the signs of the Zodiac in the sky."

We KNEW we were best and we wanted to deploy the things which had made us the best across the globe. The Church of England, public school education, Oxbridge, Parliamentary democracy, The City and London's Stock Exchange. These were the things our Victorian ancestors were so comfortably certain had made Britain great, and were therefore the things we should – relatively altruistically – export to our colonies (in return, we should be ready to admit, for the natural resources which made Britain the richest nation in the world). Those were the things which were good and true and proper. And they set off round the world with a truly missionary zeal to impose those things on people hitherto less fortunate than ourselves.

There was something of that colonialist zeal apparent in Afghanistan on several visits I made to our troops there. The original justification for our invasion and for the subsequent ten years of warfare was of course clear. Al Q'aida had carried out the greatest ever terrorist outrage on 9/11, and they needed to both be punished for it and prevented from doing anything similar ever again. For the Americans, it was a Pearl Harbour moment, shattering their illusion that the Homeland was secure. But we should never forget that 67 Britons were killed in the Twin Towers, and that the Al Q'aida threat to the UK mainland was just as real and immediate as to America. So the moral and legal justification for the invasion of Afghanistan in 2003 and the hounding of Osama Bin Laden and AQ, their removal from Afghanistan, and, to an extent, their hounding into Pakistan – is quite easily justified from whichever angle you look at it.

Afghanistan visits in 2007 and 2008.

Yet it is a mystery how we allowed that perfectly justifiable international and military ambition to transmogrify itself into a wholly unjustified and unjustifiable invasion of Iraq. Saddam Hussein, of course, was opposed to the Islamic Fundamentalists. UBL and AQ had no toe-hold in Iraq, who therefore shouldered no responsibility for 9/11. There were, of course, no weapons of mass destruction, nor could Iraq have been shown to be any kind of direct or immediate threat to the West. I remember Jack Straw desperately 'clutching at straws' to try to justify Iraq. "They stone prostitutes in the streets," I remember him saying at one time, blithely ignoring the fact that even were that true (and obviously disgraceful) it would not of itself be a justification under international law for an aggressive military invasion.

"We are with you whatever" must be Blair's (Chilcot quoted) strategic epitaph. He had no clue at all what we were doing, but he was determined to do it anyhow.

But in another way that episode is symptomatic or illustrative of something deeper. We really have very little idea of who we are, or what we are for, or what is our place in the world.

We know that we are different to the rest of the world. We secretly believe that we are better than the rest of the world, but would not be so ill-mannered as to say so, or at least we don't normally.

Our feelings of 'difference' to the rest of the world lie at the heart of the uneasy relationship we had with the other EU countries throughout our foty-year membership of the Common Market, EEC and EU. Europe, after all, is a nice place where we go on holiday. We enjoy their cultures and their wines, but they are at the end of the day, 'foreigners'. And we most certainly (as we demonstrated in the EU Referendum) are not a part of it. Nor are we the 51st state of the US, despite some arch-Eurosceptics wishing that we were. Most people probably prefer the Commonwealth to the EU, and secretly suspect that America – nice place as it is – would have been a great deal better if they had not left us.

We are ready to accept our moral obligations in the wider world, still being of the view that we are and should be amongst the top nations. It may be fashionable to decry the size of our overseas aid budget, and to call for our troops to be brought home. Yet in the stillness of the night we know it is right to be helping out people who are less fortunate than we are and to use our military might (such as it is) as a force for good in less civilised areas of the world.

It is striking, for example, how very generous we are as soon as there is some international emergency – a tsunami or earthquake, say. And our passionate support for our armed forces – the Royal Wootton Bassett effect – is second to none. Threatened government cuts to defence spending are treated with greater disdain than almost any other. "Who knows what the world will be like in ten years' time.... We couldn't do a Falklands taskforce today you know..." is the general tenor of chat, no matter how pacifist we might like to think of ourselves as being.

Our influence in the world is plain to see. Our language vies with Mandarin and Portuguese as the largest spoken language on the globe; and it being the normal language for Tim Berners-Lee's internet, my suspicion is that within a hundred years or so it will be truly the global lingua franca – the universal language of the human race. Our empire may well have had its downsides, and it is deeply unfashionable and politically incorrect to speak well of it. But very large parts of the globe got their education, their businesses, their infrastructure of roads, bridges, drains, hospitals and schools, their systems of government from the British Empire. And I suspect that at least some of them look back nostalgically to the good times they had under we British, and are glad to remain part of the Commonwealth, or British Commonwealth as it used to be (perfectly accurately) known with the Queen at its head.

Our Foreign Office was – at least until Mr Blair got his hands on it – one of the finest organisations of world diplomacy. It was an intellectual power-house second to none working the secret ways of diplomacy for peace and democracy wherever it could, and using the best British brains, training, natural decency, and ability at foreign languages to do so. William Hague was committed to returning the FCO to its former glory, and went some way towards doing so. We are leading members of NATO, one of five permanent members of the UN Security Council, members of G 8, G20 and every other international and diplomatic body which exists in the world.

We are the only nation which both spends the NATO determined 2% of GDP on defence and 0.7% of GDP on overseas aid (more about that later).

In every sense, we are acknowledged to be in the world's Premier League of Nations. Let us never forget it. And let us use that status and capability for the good of the people of the world.

8. Britain Rules the Mercantile Waves

"You were greatly offended with me for having called you a nation of shopkeepers. Had I meant by this, that you were a nation of cowards, you would have had reason to be displeased; even though it were ridiculous and contrary to historical facts; but no such thing was ever intended. I meant that you were a nation of merchants, and that all your great riches, and your grand resources arose from commerce, which is true. What else constitutes the riches of England. It is not extent of territory, or a numerous population. It is not mines of gold, silver, or diamonds. Moreover, no man of sense ought to be ashamed of being called a shopkeeper."

(Napoleon)

All of Britain's wealth; all of Britain's greatness; all of Britain's glory came from our unique world role as a maritime trading nation. Our greatness in the future – if we are to achieve it post-Brexit – will also come from trade, commerce and a global economy.

All of our historic wealth and prosperity comes from international trade, and it must now do so once again. So can we? And if so how?

Well to start us off, here are some fascinating statistics collated by Raymond Lockey, former Special Adviser to the President of the US, and Liaison to US Congress (in an unpublished blog).

"Britain is set to have the largest economy in Europe in the next fifteen years," he says, *"and be richer than America."* He then compares statistics like Current Account balance per capita, GDP Real Growth rate, the composition of GDP by industrial sectors; Government spending on Research and Development; technological achievement (the UK is 7th in the world), tax payments, Gross Savings, Gross Fixed Capital Formation (I wish I knew what that was); oil production and a host of other similar economic and trade statistics, which he then compares with the US, China, India and other Global powers and super-powers.

He concludes: *"Economic Power is one element of consideration in determining 'super power' status. On a per capita basis, the UK often either ties or bests the United States.... Another, also within the realms of 'soft power' is the strength, depth and width of a country's financial and capital markets... London is a world leader in that area... and Brexit {may} unhook her from the restraints of the EU...{and} prompt a new renaissance of the financial markets operating out of London... My guess is that being unhinged from the over-reaching restrictions imposed by the European Parliament will offer the UK the opportunity to expand to even greater lengths than remaining in the EU.*

Another element… is the productivity of the workforce, the innovations of its joint higher education institutions and research centers. In both {the UK} is also a world leader."

Mr Lockey's optimistic assessment of Britain's economic future is very much supported by a more recent Henry Jackson Society report, "The Audit of Geopolitical Capability". This study rigorously evaluated Britain's standing using thirty-five indicators, comparing us with seven other major powers – China, France, Germany, India, Japan, Russia and the United States. The categories analysed included economics, technological prowess, military strength and cultural prestige. As the report's author, Dr Alan Mendoza, concludes: "For all the doom and gloom surrounding the implications of Brexit, the reality shines through that Britain remains a leading global power nation with immense soft and hard power capabilities. The lesson of this report is clear: Our future is what we choose to make of it."

Now it is perfectly true that our manufacturing base, and our non-financial balance of payments as a result, is woefully inadequate. That is the case now, and will remain the case post-Brexit. It was always said that we owed our nineteenth century economic dominance to the ability to make things and export them overseas, using our empire as a source of raw materials as well as a market for manufactured goods. If you don't make things, the Boy's Book of Basic Economics would say, then you cannot prosper.

Yet unless we tried to rebalance the vast wage and raw materials imbalance in the world, there is really no likelihood of our ever returning to being a world producer of manufactured goods. I very much welcome the decent levels of pay we have now achieved for all in the UK. It is right that people earn enough to have a decent life, and I for one would never want to see us go back to the low wage economy of the 'fifties and 'sixties, far less the extreme poverty economy of the nineteenth century. No matter how lowly your work, or your training and education, you can expect to earn a minimum of £10 an hour, which is by no means generous, but is well above poverty wages.

What's more, thanks to prosperous businesses and a decent economy, most people today have a reasonable expectation of employment, and employment at a fair level of income and allowing a fair way of life. The OECD estimate the average annual wage in Britain to be equivalent to $42,390, the seventeenth highest in the world. The equivalent in Turkey is $11,180; in China it's $8260; in Thailand $5640; in the Philippines, $3580; Vietnam $2050; India $1680; Bangladesh $1330, or the Democratic Republic of the Congo $400. It is perhaps hardly surprising that we cannot compete in low-skilled manufacturing. Were we to seek to do so, we would also be returning a large part of our own population to poverty, degradation and filth.

The Dyson manufacturers of bagless vacuum cleaners in my own North Wiltshire constituency are a fair exemplar. It used to be – twenty years ago – that they not only designed and invented electrical goods in Malmesbury, but they also clipped the plastic together on a supply line. That ended about fifteen years ago or so, when the main manufacturing effort was transferred to Indonesia. I am glad to say that Dyson then switched to high-end engineering and design in Malmesbury, and now employ 3000 highly skilled, and doubtless very highly paid, individuals, with a consequent benefit to the local economy. Sir James Dyson is now planning a design and engineering college, and is redeveloping the old Air Force base at Hullavington, at vast expense, to house it. Sir James has for long been deeply concerned about the lack of engineering and design expertise emerging from our schools and universities, and has acted to help correct that deficit.

The young Mr Dyson invented bagless vacuum cleaners after observing how inefficient a cleaner was the old kind. He developed it into a multi-million pound business, developing many other things such as the Dyson hand-drier and fan along the away. He moved his basic manufacturing to a low-wage economy in the Far East, from whence he imports under WTO terms to most of Europe, making a healthy profit as he does so. The UK

With Sir James Dyson and PM David Cameron.

supplies the expertise, the training, the inventing, the designing; the Far East provides the muscle. That seems to me to be a perfectly reasonable deal.

Incidentally, Dyson argue that they trade perfectly happily with the EU from their manufacturing base in the Far East, and that they need no EU Trade agreement to do so. "We make first class products, which we sell at an affordable price. We need no government interference to achieve that," is broadly the argument. Sir James is an outspoken critic of the EU as a result – not least because many of their interferingly bossy directives would have made it impossible for him to sell his appliances across the Continent of Europe. He is an outspoken supporter of Brexit as being just what business needs.

Not only does the Dyson example help the UK economy; it is also of course enormously beneficial to the Indonesian economy, where people who would otherwise presumably not be employed at all are given decent jobs at reasonable wages.

Having said all of that, there are of course many manufacturing capabilities which we should always seek to keep onshore. We have a particular expertise in high tech manufacturing, and in the defence sector. We must keep that here both because of National Intellectual Property, the need to be able to defend our shores without undue reliance on overseas nations; and also because we have developed a first-class export competence in the defence sector. Airbus may be a European collaboration (despite the fact that such collaborations very rarely work), yet their high-tech factory manufacturing wings for their aircraft at Filton near Bristol, is an outstanding example of what we can do in the UK. And despite mutterings off, Airbus are showing no real signs of reducing their investment in the UK post-Brexit. The same, of course, could be said of BAE Systems, Rolls Royce, and American companies based in the UK, like Raytheon and Boeing.

I was glad to play a small part in securing a recent deal under which a multi-national US technology company purchased a 250-person business in Calne in my constituency some time after Brexit had been announced. It was a multi-million-pound deal which came about as a result of, not despite Brexit. "We wanted a toe-hold in the European Market," they told me, "and we see real benefits of being outside the EU, whose regulatory regime can be stifling." Near Europe, but not run by it was the broad theme.

Our small and medium sized businesses, few of which have any trade relationship with the EU, may therefore be amongst the clearest beneficiaries of our leaving.

There are 5.4 million businesses in the UK, 99% of them employing up to 250 people, 5.1 million of them being micro businesses employing fewer than 9 people (and totalling 15.6 million, or 60% of all those employed). A further 4.8 million people are self-employed (or 15% of all workers in the UK). Very few of them, of course, export to the EU, or anywhere else for that matter. Yet all are subject to every rule, regulation, bureaucracy, health and safety and general irritation which can be thought up both by national and local government, and especially by the EU. I was talking to a restaurant manager the other day locally. She said that two thirds of her time is now taken up with rules and regulations, HR stuff, health and safety, tax and trading returns, VAT and the rest of it. She's a chef, but says she spends hardly any time in the kitchen anymore because of it.

So I hope that we will make good use of the Brexit negotiations to sweep away swathes of regulations and bureaucracy coming from the EU. That should, I hope, be fairly easy. But let's also use the opportunity to free up businesses, large and small alike. Let's relieve self-employed people of these burdens wherever they may originate. Schools should be places where people teach, and restaurants where they serve delicious meals. Farms should be places where they grow produce, and factories where they make things. Let us free up our people to get on with the things they are good at.

Despite the inevitable downturn in the heavy end of manufacturing (shipbuilding, steel, coal), the UK also has an enormous amount to offer in the higher end of design and engineering, and complex high value manufacturing.

The empire was built – and the post-Brexit new Britain will be built – on much more than manufacturing. We were a trading nation. Our traders like the Hong Kong companies, Swire and Jardine Matheson, bought and sold commodities and goods all round the world, shipped them to where they needed to be and sold them again. I spent ten years as a shipbroker, arranging the carriage of large quantities of coal and iron ore from the US to Japan for smelting, of hundreds of thousands of tonnes of wheat from Australia to the Middle East, of sulphur from Vancouver to India. It was carried on Greek-owned ships, registered in Panama, with Indian crewmen. Each deal would be worth tens of millions of pounds, financed from the Square Mile, the commodities traded there, the ships fixed and the insurances covered all within a few hundred yards of each other. It was British expertise, capital, free markets, education and traditions, as well as our law, convenient time-zone, and City of London institutions like the Commodity Exchange, the Stock Exchange, Lloyds, the Baltic Exchange, Trinity House and of course the largest conglomeration of banks in the world which made all of that possible. And the main elements of it still exist today.

English commercial law is the best in the world; *Our Word Our Bond* traditions in the Baltic Shipping Exchange and the Stock Exchange; the maritime expertise of Trinity House; the liquidity of Lloyds, and the sheer quantity of capital available is what makes the City what it is. And it brings vast wealth to the UK as a result. We must preserve and nurture and expand all of that capability post-Brexit.

I was one of those who deeply regretted the Blairite destruction of the Royal Yacht *Britannia* – that magnificent symbol of all that is great about Britain. I would be glad to see a new Royal Yacht commissioned, as is being proposed in some quarters. What could be finer than a new *Britannia* sailing into some foreign

Royal Yacht Britannia, *6 March 1963.*

55

port Red Ensign flying, for a Royal reception on board, the magnificent band of the Royal Marines Beating Retreat as the sun sinks behind an overseas horizon. What a great symbol of post-Brexit British strength that would be.

Britain has the Intellectual Property, intelligence, managerial skills, universities, training, history, time zone, innovation, entrepreneurial spirit, inventiveness, design and manufacturing capabilities combined with the Protestant work ethic to be once again one of greatest economic and trading of all nations.

Now with all of that as background, there are those who would nonetheless argue that we put it at risk by leaving the EU. They would say that the EU, especially the Single Market and the Customs Union, is the modern trading equivalent of the British Empire, without which we cannot hope to prosper. That would be perfectly true if by some ridiculous means we were post-Brexit to become wholly cut off from our trading partners on the mainland of Europe. But no-one except the most extreme 'Remainer' polemicists has ever suggested such a thing. Of course we will continue to trade fully with the EU countries. That is massively in their interests as well as ours. The concept of Bastion UK, with our drawbridge drawn up trading only with the rest of the world, but excluding France and Germany, is so ludicrous as to be unworthy of print or of refutation. There may well be some posturing, some tough negotiating, perhaps some hiccups along the way. But what is for sure is that in a few years' time (if not immediately), our trading relationship with the other European countries will be just as good, perhaps a great deal better post-Brexit than it was before we left.

Let me quote in extenso from an article by Andrew Sentance, Senior Economic Adviser at accounting and management giants PwC, and a former member of the Bank of England's Monetary Policy Committee, written in November 2016, long after the decision to leave the EU had been taken.

"UK export performance since 2007 appears to have been stronger outside the EU than within the single market... The UK also has a strong comparative advantage in services trade which is growing more strongly globally than trade in goods. Medium-term growth prospects remain strong in key emerging market regions, including Asia, Africa and the Middle East... UK export growth to markets outside the EU should soon resume momentum. The key policy priorities for improving UK trade prospects after Brexit should be: securing the best possible access to the Single Market; a programme of trade promotion in non-EU markets; supply-side reform; and active engagement with the major international institutions – including the World Trade Organisation. New Free Trade Agreements with countries outside the EU will take a long time to secure and are therefore likely to offer only limited benefits to the UK in the immediate aftermath of Brexit."

The rest of the document is published in the UK Economic Outlook paper of November 2016, and is to be commended and recommended for its clarity and even-handedness. Another seminal work was an article by Peter Lilley in the *Daily Telegraph* on 26 May 2016 (i.e. before the Referendum outcome).

"How important are Trade Deals? It pains me {as a former Secretary of State for Trade

and Industry}, to admit that their importance is grossly exaggerated. Countries succeed with or without trade deals, if they produce goods and services other countries want. (The Dyson argument.) *Tariffs between developed counties now average low single figures – small beer by comparison with recent movements in exchange rates. The most worthwhile trading agreements are with fast-growing developing countries which still have high tariffs.*

Is our £10 Billion net contribution to the EU a price worth paying for tariff free access to the EU market? If we left the EU with no trade deal – inconceivable as that is – our exports would face tariffs averaging just 2.4%. But our net contribution to the EU Budget is equivalent to a 7% tariff. Paying 7 % to avoid 2.4% costs is miss-selling that dwarfs the PPI scandal!"

Vast forests have been expended laying out the advantages and disadvantages of EU membership from a trading perspective. But surely the views of Peter Lilley (and James Dyson) prevail – that we will succeed if we make things and provide things which other countries want and need, whether within the EU or outside of it. That is the simplest basis of all international capitalist trade. It served us well for hundreds of years and can and must do so again.

Post Brexit we will be able to return to the proud and independent trading nation we once were. Is it not absurd that we are not allowed under EU rules to discuss our trading relationship with any other nation in the world? That must be done through the EU, and woe betide any nation that tries to do it independently. We have even been told that during the two-year period during which Article 50 (the means of our departure from the EU) is debated and discussed we may not seek to form a clear trading relationship except via EU machinery. What nonsense. What arrogance, that is, and I very much hope that we start with no further delay to discuss how our businesses can buy and sell things round the world after we have freed ourselves from the artificial shackles of the EU.

Even more absurd is the notion that we may not at the moment be members of the World Trade Organisation. Surely agreeing how we trade with the rest of the world is an absolutely essential part of nationhood? Incidentally the scare-mongers who predict that the Article 50 negotiations will all end in a disaster and we 'will have to fall back up on the WTO terms' are surely missing the point. Most of our trade today is and always has been done on WTO terms. The only trade which is done differently is that with other EU countries. We trade with America, Japan, India, Australia, Africa on WTO terms, as does every other EU nation. It is not such a catastrophe. Dyson, for example, make the point that the bulk of their exports are already on WTO terms. Indeed, since their main manufacturing base is in Indonesia, every single Dyson vacuum cleaner, hand drier, fan or hairdryer is, and always has been, sold within the EU on WTO terms. That holds no terror for them.

As we leave the EU, we will be moving from a rich man's club, under which we abdicate our freedoms and sovereignty in favour of the lowest common denominator across the Continent of Europe in favour of being a strong and independent trading nation (as we always were throughout history). We will be competing economically with the Far East on the one hand and the US on the other as an independent economic powerhouse. We will use our wit, our language, our law and our banking system to trade independently with both gigantic economic superstates.

Britain must be both free – and as a result – economically strong. Both will be the most direct consequence of Brexit.

9. Britain and the Polar Regions

"Had we lived, I should have had a tale to tell of the hardihood, endurance, and courage of my companions which would have stirred the heart of every Englishman. These rough notes and our dead bodies must tell the tale."

(Captain Scott)

The essential outward looking, maritime spirit which made Britain great is perhaps exemplified in one (perhaps otherwise lamentably obscure) area of our Foreign Policy. There is an enormously dedicated and successful department in the FCO, headed by a committed official called Jane Rumble for a great many years, called the Polar Regions Department. Its task (and Jane has made it her own – it should be recognised by a Polar medal at very least) is to watch over Britain's relations with Antarctica (where, as a signatory to the Antarctic Treaty we have an essential diplomatic role) and – perhaps more recently – the Arctic.

It is curious that despite the northernmost tip of Shetland being only 400 or so

Scott at work in his cabin, Antarctica, 1913.

miles away from the Arctic, it is only now with the commercial, fishing, tourism and mineral possibilities being increasingly offered to Britain by the retreating ice, we are at last taking our relations with our near neighbours in the Arctic at all seriously.

Inspired by my friends, polar explorer, mountaineer, adventurer, Sir David Hempleman-Adams, and Swedish philanthropist, Frederik Paulsen (the only human to have reached all eight – yes eight – Poles), I have been lucky enough to do a fair bit of travelling (as a tourist) in these remote and chilly places. As a result, I have begun to shake Parliament out of its Polar slumber, and establish some understanding of our duties to the Poles and the opportunities which the Arctic in particular offers us.

Brexit will, I hope, increase our interest in the Poles, our understanding of and determination to do something about climate change; and our willingness to guide sustainable and careful exploitation of all they have to offer.

The tale of Britain's engagement with the North and South Poles is a curious and patchy one. My friend, Dr Duncan Depledge, who is Secretary of the Parliamentary Polar Group, and largely responsible for its huge success in recent years has been kind enough to sketch it out for us.

At the end of the fifteenth century, England was a middling power in northern Europe, dwarfed by the might of the Spanish and Portuguese Empires. Although Henry VII rejected the terms of the Treaty of Tordesillas in 1494, he was in no position to contest Spanish and Portuguese control of the South Atlantic trade routes and the New World. As the English geographer, Roger Barlow, wrote in 1541, the *"waie of the orient"* and the *"waie of occident"* had been blocked. England, would have to find the *"waie of the northe"* if it was to be able to establish a trade route to the riches in Asia, break Spanish and Portuguese domination, and create an empire of its own.

Could it be that the foundations of the British Empire were in fact forged in the heroic search for a new trade route to Asia through the frozen and desolate wastes of the icy north? After all, before Henry VII commissioned the Genoese navigator, John Cabot, in 1496 to cross the Atlantic and search for the Northwest Passage, English maritime activity had largely been constricted to fishing off the coast of Iceland (although some would argue that English maritime prowess acquired in these waters, paved the way for the first crossings of the North Atlantic). Henry VII understood that the only way that England could break out of these confines was to discover a way out of the North Atlantic through the Arctic. With it would come new territories and the resources that would allow him to break southern European monopolies.

Cabot's voyage across the Atlantic was just the beginning of what would become a centuries-long obsession for the English. Wave after wave of expeditions followed. All were either lost to the ice, or turned back. Yet the discoveries that these explorers made still proved crucial to the realisation of England's ambitions to become a global power.

Cabot himself discovered Newfoundland, opening the door to the establishment of the earliest English settlements abroad and laying the foundations for future expansion in North America. Half a century later, his son Sebastian, together with Hugh Willoughby and Richard Chancellor went in search of a Northeast Passage in the icy waters north of Russia. They failed, and Willoughby and his crew perished in the ice.

Chancellor, though, survived and found himself in the court of Ivan the Terrible, with whom he reached an agreement to establish a new trade route between England and the embryonic Russian state. He returned to England and created the Muscovy Company. It was the first ever joint-stock trading company, the Crown granting it a monopoly on all trade with Russia, it thereby becoming the precursor to the East India Company (formed in 1600) and the Hudson's Bay Company (1670). The latter of course served as the vanguard in the expansion of English, and later British, colonial rule in North America and the former in Asia.

It was in the Arctic that the English also discovered their hunger for whale and seal products. In the sixteenth century, the Muscovy Company found whaling and sealing grounds around Spitsbergen and soon entered into fierce competition with other nations for control over these precious resources, which paved the way for a massive increase in the use of whale and seal products in everyday life. In the centuries that followed, whale bone, whale oil and baleen were used in everything from lamp-lighting to machine lubricants, to soaps, paints, dress hoops and corsets. Hundreds of ships and thousands of men from more than thirty cities were employed in the whaling industry, creating huge pools of experienced sailors that could be pressed into service by the Royal Navy.

The English insatiable appetite for whales and seals also took sailors south. In 1773 Captain James Cook made the first recorded crossing of the Antarctic Circle while searching for the Southern Continent aboard HMS *Resolution*. Although he failed to discover Antarctica, his reports that the Southern Ocean was abundant with whales and seals attracted great interest back home. Subsequent expeditions led by James Weddell and James Clark Ross, among others, opened up Antarctica and the sub-Antarctic islands, and were to a large extent driven by commercial interests associated with the discovery of new hunting grounds.

Yet the biggest prize on offer – a maritime passageway to Asia – continued to elude the English, so much so that even religious and moral convictions were put to the test. In 1595, one of Elizabeth I's chief navigators, John Davis, claimed that God would never withhold the Arctic Ocean from the English by freezing it, and consequently it must be navigable.

In 1816, John Barrow, the Second Secretary to the Admiralty, believed that the very supremacy of the British Empire would be threatened if it was not the first to discover the Northwest Passage. He turned to the surpluses of ships and officers left at his disposal after the Napoleonic Wars to drive forward a new wave of exploration in the Arctic which would further the scientific knowledge of the nation and open up new commercial opportunities. However, the succession of voyages that followed all met with failure, culminating in the disastrous loss of Sir John Franklin and his crew in 1847. Although the Northwest Passage was in fact found (by Robert McClure) during attempts to discover Franklin's fate, it was unnavigable, seemingly confirming that the Arctic could never be assimilated into the British Empire.

Interest subsequently turned to Antarctica. Antarctica of course is a continent and not an ocean and so would perhaps be easier to assimilate into the British Empire, despite its extreme environment and remoteness from the rest of the world. The first major British expedition there – the British Antarctic Expedition – was launched in 1898, setting in motion the chain of events which would make, each in their own way, Robert Falcon Scott and Ernest Shackleton the new heroes of British polar exploration.

"For scientific leadership give me Scott; for swift and efficient travel, Amundsen; but when you are in a hopeless situation, when there seems to be no way out, get on your knees and pray for Shackleton." (Sir Raymond Priestley)

"Men wanted for hazardous journey. Small wages, bitter cold, long months of complete darkness, constant danger, safe return doubtful. Honour and recognition in case of success." (Ernest Shackleton. Probably fake newspaper announcement before his *Endurance* expedition.)

Disappointed and defeated, Scott and team at the South Pole.

But if the nineteenth century was an age of heroic exploration in the polar regions, the twentieth century forced Britain to factor the Arctic and Antarctica into its geopolitical calculations. During the First World War, Britain stationed forces in Archangel and Murmansk in the Russian Arctic to support the White Army, where they remained until 1919. In the Second World War, Britain returned to the Arctic theatre again as it fought another 'Forgotten War' alongside Norway and the Soviet Union to prevent Germany from gaining control of crucial ports and threatening Trans-Atlantic sea lanes. Only recently were veterans of the 'Arctic Convoys' that kept supply lines from the North Atlantic to the Soviet Union intact finally honoured with a campaign medal of their own.

During the Cold War, the strategic importance of the Arctic grew still further as the United States and Russia faced off over the icy wastes. Arctic routes were by far the shortest for long-range bombers and intercontinental ballistic missiles to reach major population centres and key strategic assets on both sides. Later, under the ice, British, US and Soviet submarines bristling with nuclear armaments engaged in games of hide and seek to try to gain a first-strike advantage.

In Antarctica, meanwhile, a different kind of game unfolded in the post-war years. Britain had reasserted its sovereignty over the Falkland Islands in 1833. In 1908, the British Government extended its territorial claims in the South Atlantic to include South Georgia, the South Orkneys, the South Shetlands, and the South Sandwich Islands (also known as the Falkland Islands Dependencies). Britain's expanded claim also included Graham's Land, the portion of the Antarctic Peninsula that lies closest to South America. But in the 1930s, Britain faced the first intrusions from Argentina and Chile which also claimed Graham's Land and established rival bases on nearby Deception Island.

An increase in Argentine incursions into Britain's relatively undefended South Atlantic Empire during the Second World War led the Government to launch a secret mission to build the first permanent British bases in Antarctica. But neither the Argentines nor the Chileans were to be put off, and Anglo-Argentine-Chilean tensions continued to simmer after the Second World War. By then though, the United States and Russia also had designs on Antarctica.

Geopolitical ambitions (and conflict) in Antarctica would have been expensive, as well as largely unproductive, and so in 1959 the seven 'claimant states' (Britain, Argentina, Chile, Norway and France, as well as newly independent New Zealand and Australia) together with the United States, the Soviet Union, Belgium, South Africa and Japan, signed the Antarctic Treaty, to demilitarise Antarctica and suspend all territorial claims there in the interest of promoting international scientific cooperation. In the years since, the Antarctic Treaty has grown into the Antarctic Treaty System comprising the original treaty and several other protocols and conventions that seek to enhance environment protection and conservation, while preventing damaging extractive activities such as mining.

Although the world has changed dramatically since the age of heroic exploration, Britain is still a major player in both the Arctic and Antarctica.

In the south, Britain, as a 'claimant state', still has responsibility for ensuring rules and regulations relating to the Antarctic Treaty System are enforced in the British Antarctic Territory. The Royal Naval patrol ship HMS *Protector* helps police maritime activity in the Southern Ocean (where Britain is responsible for around 1.5 million square km of waters). Britain is a major contributor to Antarctic science. There are more than 200 scientists in UK universities and research centres – with the world-class British Antarctic Survey leading the way – undertaking frontier science in Antarctica. Britain also continues to be a leader in negotiations among consultative parties to the Antarctic Treaty on issues such as the establishment of Marine Protected Areas around Antarctica, tourism, the management of historical sites, and education. The science Britain does in Antarctica, second only to the United States, also contributes to our understanding of global issues such as climate change, food security, innovation and economic growth.

HMS Protector *in the Antarctic.*

In the north, it has been more than century since Britain gave up its last claims to Arctic territory, yet its huge science capability matters there too. Britain was there from the start when the international community came together towards the end of the Cold War to establish a set of new institutions such as the International Arctic Science Committee, and later the Arctic Council, that have gone on to strengthen cooperation on science, environmental protection and sustainable development in the region.

Currently, there are more than 75 UK universities and research institutes that are involved or involved in Arctic research. In 2011, there were more than 500 UK scientists with Arctic-related research interests (double the number working in Antarctica), ranging from those seeking to better understand what role the Arctic plays in global atmospheric, oceanic, and climatic processes, to those monitoring changes in marine and terrestrial ecosystems, to those developing Britain's world-leading capabilities in autonomous systems. Between 2006 and 2015, the UK ranked fourth in terms of its outputs of scientific papers on the Arctic, and sixth for impact, but among non-Arctic states it was first in terms of both number of research projects and funding.

With a new world-class ice-strengthened polar research vessel, the RSS *Sir David Attenborough*, due to begin operation in 2019, Britain is likely to remain a leading polar science nation for the foreseeable future.

I very much enjoyed leading a group of UK Parliamentarians to visit the most northerly inhabited spot on the Globe at Ny Alesund in Svalbardin 2017. It is an international research station, originally established by the British, who still play a leading role in it. At 79 degrees north, it is but a few hundred miles from the Pole itself and offers an unparalleled research capability, not least because of the purity of the atmosphere, and of the flora and fauna.

Britain has played a historically gigantic role at both North and South Poles. The retreating ice – regret it as we may – offers unparalleled new opportunities in the Arctic, and we are well placed to play a leading role in them. There are also developing new military threats in the north, with Russia showing a real interest in once again dominating the supply routes from the USA to Europe, especially using submarines.

I hope that our key role and interest in the Poles may be a good exemplar of a new approach by Britain to the world post-Brexit. We will no longer be a member of a small and introverted group of rich countries examining our collective navels. We can once again be a great and outward looking maritime nation ready to contribute to – and benefit from – a much wider world.

10. Power Through Overseas Aid

"Foreign aid goes from poor people in rich countries to rich people in poor countries." (Rand Paul)

O r does it? Rand Paul's famous quote had some merit in the days when we (and even more so the EU) paid vast amounts of money to (often corrupt) overseas governments. That has largely ended, with most money now going directly to particular overseas projects very often via Non Governmental Organisations like Save the Children, Oxfam, Christian Aid.

After Trade, one of the most visible – and perhaps effective – forms of 'soft power' – (and feasibly a covert route to greatness) – is power delivered through our massive Overseas Aid programmes.

We need to understand and agree whether our world-view and our aid ambitions are motivated entirely by self-interest – the best interests of the 65 million people within our shores, or whether we have some wider duty to the world – and the poor and starving, the oppressed and enslaved? I am proud of the fact that we Brits spend 0.7% of our Gross Domestic Product on overseas aid. It's a noble achievement just for humanitarian post-imperialist reasons. One billion people go to bed starving, while another million go to bed bloated. Five million children die of starvation in the world every year, while we think nothing of throwing away a vast tonnage of half-eaten food. Thousands of people around the world are dying of thirst, while we in the West think nothing of leaving the taps running to fill up our swimming pools. That can't be right, and there seems to me an urgent and inescapable moral imperative to do what we can to help.

In trying to map out what the twenty-first century holds for us, surely seeking to eradicate world poverty, starvation, aids, and thirst must be somewhere pretty high up the British agenda for pure humanitarian motives. But there are also sound *strategic* reasons for it. Nearly every war in history (leaving aside those caused by religion) has been caused by poverty. Either the peoples of the aggressing country are in dire economic straits (as was the case, for example, with Nazi Germany), or the aggressor sees easy pickings in poverty-stricken neighbouring states (Nazi Germany and much of Russia's aggression under the Soviet Union). By contrast, the likelihood of warfare or tension between neighbouring states whose people are well fed is pretty remote.

The argument that the EU has a war-avoiding role to play, then, is only true in the sense that if all European states are rich and prosperous there is little likelihood of them falling out with each other. State on State European war now seems an ancient worry – France is no more likely to invade Spain than we would be to invade France. Yet where an EU country is bankrupt and its people poor, the likelihood is that much greater. Is strife between Greece and Turkey impossible? Might there not be a risk of further economic or racial strife in the Balkans? Are we certain that there is no risk to Georgia, Azerbaijan (which is close to being European) or Romania?

Those risks are not ameliorated by fake political structures like the EU, which might actually exacerbate them. They are better avoided by finding ways of eradicating poverty and making sure that bellies are well filled. The same of course applies in spades elsewhere round the world. Is there any likelihood of China and Japan going to war? None whatsoever. But what about China and Nepal? What about India and Pakistan over Kashmir? What about North Korea, whose extreme poverty and subjugation of her citizens may play a part in her global nuclear ambitions)? Large parts of Africa are more or less constantly at war; Sri Lanka is only now bravely trying to recover from it; much of South America teeters on the brink from time to time.

All of that warfare strife and tension comes from poverty and starvation. That great book (whose predictions thankfully never came to pass) General Sir John Hackett's *Third World War*, convincingly argued that eventually the Soviet Union would become aggressive towards the West simply to assuage the inward-looking anger of its poor (an argument which President Putin knows very well.) His logic applies so well to most (but not all) warfare.

The risk of an uprising against the world's rich by the world's poor is, if anything, exacerbated by one development since the General's time – the Internet.

For the first time in history people of even the most extreme poverty and disadvantage have an easy way of seeing what the rest of the world is like – TV and even more so the Internet. That has the obvious effect of increasing envy of others' good fortune. It also has the malign effect of raising false expectations. Everyone in the world now expects to have a car, mobile phone, deep freeze, and designer clothes and a general lifestyle to go with those things. The resentment at not having those things is made all the worse by that awareness.

Poverty, starvation and thirst; the global and the local environment in all of its guises; and religion. What a toxic mix the three of them are.

Yet more than anything else they are things we can actually do something about.

Refusing aid (physical aid or reconstruction) to the world's poorest countries would be positively Billy Bunter refusing to share his sandwich with Oliver Twist in the corner of the playground. It would only be a matter of time before Billy could expect a jolly good scragging. The West, not least the EU, is, in my view, looking increasingly Bunter-esque.

We are still the fourth richest country in the world, at least some of that wealth deriving – in an ancestral sense – from our ruthless extraction of natural resources (including human beings as slaves) from large parts of the globe over two centuries or more. Even were that not so, as the fourth largest economy in the world, do we not as human beings have a moral imperative to do what we can to help those less fortunate than ourselves? Massive overseas aid is – and has been for much of our post-imperialist lives – a central part of our liberal, 'caring' approach to the world. And quite right too.

Yet if it were just about Humanitarian Relief, there would be some justification in the oft-repeated mantra 'Charity begins at home.' "Why should it be," my constituents sometimes ask, "that we are helping poor people overseas, helping with education, looking after the disabled when we do such an inadequate job here at home. Why are my taxes being used in rich countries (sometimes even our enemies), like China, or India, when we are closing schools, and patients in Accident and Emergency Departments wait for hours on trollies before they are treated?" Now there is a degree of strength in that argument (even although it ignores the fundamental inequalities which exist even if our public services are less good than we would like them to be. Most inhabitants of most of the rest of the world would give their eye teeth for the healthcare, education, social care and benefits and the rest of it which we enjoy in this – rather ungrateful – part of the world.) The fact is that no matter how liberal or 'caring' we may be about poverty, starvation and ignorance in the rest of the world, it will still not convince many of our fellow countrymen of the innate benefits of feeding the world's poor and starving. They just do not buy it (especially the more rabid UKIP wing of modern-day British thought).

A much better way of persuading them of the benefit of the 0.7% of GDP which we spend overseas, is that that money is of direct benefit to us at home. That also happens to be one of the most important reasons for it.

For example, we all well remember the catastrophic floods which occurred in Pakistan in 2010. Approximately one fifth of the Pakistani mainland was flooded; roughly 20 million people were affected by them in one way or another, and there was a death toll of close to 2000. The UN Secretary General Ban Ki-Moon, asked for $460 million in emergency relief, commenting that it was the worst disaster he had ever seen. But after a month or so only 20% of that figure had appeared. The World Health Organisation reported that ten million people were drinking unsafe water; there was $4billion worth of damage to structures, and over $500million damage to crops. The total economic impact was estimated to be as much as £43billion. The entire Indus Valley from the Afghan border to Karachi was devastated. Not only was all of this a human and economic catastrophe. It also had real potential security consequences. The Pakistani military forces, especially in the north west of the country, were diverted away from fighting the Taliban to flood relief, offering the terrorists a very welcome respite to recoup their strength, as well as leaving key target sites largely unguarded. There was also much public perception of political failures in the aftermath of the flooding. There were, as a result, insurgencies in Baluchistan and Waziristan, growing urban sectarian discord, an increase in suicide bombings, and deteriorating relations with India. The Pakistani government was blamed for a sluggish and disorganised response to the floods. That led to riots, with looting of aid convoys by hunger-stricken people. The lack of a unified government response allowed Islamicist groups such as Lashkar-e-Taiba and Jamat-e-Islami to supply their own aid with minimal resistance. In Sindh province, the ruling Pakistan People's Party ministers were accused of using their influence improperly to divert the floods away from their own properties into more densely populated areas.

In other words, there was a very real risk for two or three months of very severe political consequences. And the direct beneficiaries of that instability would be Islamic fundamentalists and terrorists, with a direct and quantifiable consequence for the West. Without exaggerating the case, there would even have been a chance of the already weakened Pakistani government collapsing, to be replaced, presumably, by an Islamicist state – the first to be in possession of nuclear weapons, with obviously chilling consequences for the world.

So the strategic and locally tactical consequences of doing nothing about the floods could well have had massive consequences for the peace and stability of the West. Relieving the suffering, and propping up the broadly friendly Pakistani government reduced the risk of an upsurge in terrorist freedoms and activity and therefore directly saved lives in the West. Britain gave £134 million to the aid effort provided by most of the rest of the world. We also brought forward a £10 million bridge project to replace some of those washed away. Private donations, coordinated by the Disasters Emergency Committee in addition totalled more than

Prime Minister David Cameron and I visit UK Aid base at Kemble Airfield, North Wiltshire.

£60 million. Interventions carried out included the flying in of 400 tonnes of aid, and providing tents, shelter kits, blankets, water containers and sanitation and nutritional interventions. Much of it was shipped from Kemble Airfield in my own constituency.

The Pakistani floods may be an especially graphic example, of a much wider real purpose behind our huge overseas aid programmes. If poverty, starvation and thirst cause instability and strife, which is nearly always to the disadvantage or risk of us in the West, then countering poverty starvation and thirst must, at least in most cases, be of fairly demonstrable and direct and quantifiable help to the peace and security of the West.

The insecurity which would be the direct result of financial inequalities between the northern hemisphere and the southern hemisphere was of course first highlighted by former German Chancellor, Willy Brandt in his 1980 report, 'North-South: A programme for Survival.' *"Could we not begin the new century by laying the basis for reasonable relations among all people and nations, and to build a world in which sharing, justice, freedom and peace might prevail?"* he asked. The Brandt Report suggested primarily that a great chasm in general standards of living had developed along the North-South Divide ('The Brandt Line') and that there should therefore be a large transfer of resources from developed to developing countries.

The Report estimated that 800 million people in the South lived in absolute poverty, some 40% of the South's population not being able to secure the most basic necessities of life. As a result, although life expectancy had improved a little in recent years, access to reasonable healthcare was still woefully inadequate; housing was appalling as a result of increasing urbanisation with two thirds of the entire population unable to secure decent housing; and education was minimalist, with 80% of the population being illiterate in 34 countries. The Report went on to argue that it was very much in the interests of the North to seek to eradicate these massive imbalances, from an economic and security standpoint. The Report also highlighted the root cause of much of this poverty – massive population growth, and correctly predicted that if it were not dealt with, then the net result would be huge migration, with resentment, social unrest and political consequences for the North.

The reality, of course, is that the recommendations in the Brandt Report were never implemented, due to the Cold War partly, and to a collective lack of political will among world leaders. The Report was updated in 2001 by James B. Quilligan, in a report entitled 'The Brandt Equation – 21st Century Blueprint for the New Global Economy.' If it were similarly to be updated today, it is pretty certain that the update would accept that much of what Brandt predicted is, as we speak, coming to pass. The inequalities between North and South are worse than ever, and the result is war, terrorism, strife, mass migration and instability.

The only serious way we can counter exactly the consequences which Brandt predicted is through our overseas aid programme. That is a lesson and a reality which Western politicians must take steps to drive home to their electorate to try to counter the rather fatuous 'charity begins at home' argument. The UK should be proud of the fact that we are the only nation in the world which achieves the UN's 0.7% of GDP in Overseas Aid as well as NATO's prescription that we should spend at least 2% of GDP on defence. That means that we more than punch our weight in the world.

There are other things we can do as back-up to our aid programme. Between now and 2050, the global population is projected to rise from a current 7 billion to 9.2 billion, demanding, according to the UN Food and Agriculture Organisation, a 60% increase in food production. Limiting population growth, and helping provide food are both within our remit and gift. 791 million people are starving, and 5 million children under the age of 5 die of malnutrition every year – 5 million children a year. Just think of it. Worse than that, 161 million children are stunted through malnutrition, 99 million are underweight, and 51 million are wasted due to acute malnutrition. Hardly surprising that they gaze longingly at Western images on the Internet and think about starting the hazardous journey to this land of milk and honey. Truly the Victorian pauper pressing his nose against the glass of the rich child's sweetie shop.

It was fascinating to visit a farm in Brazil a few years ago. "How big is your farm, then?" I rather simplistically asked the farmer. "Oh about 1 to 1.25," he said. "1 to 1.25 whats?" I enquired. "1 to 1.25 million hectares," he said pointing down the rows of soya bean the end of which we could not see because of the curvature of the earth. Three crops a year, much aided by genetic modification, his only main problem being the wild ostriches! When Brazil sorts out a few infrastructure problems (like train lines to get the crops out to the ports), they will truly be able to feed the world.

We in prosperous, North West Europe should be doing our part too. There is something positively immoral about set aside and quotas of any kind. How can we be restricting production in order to keep our prices high? How can we pay farmers to leave fields to rot when half the world is starving?

How can it be that thousands of acres of productive land, especially across the South West of England, particularly at the moment across Wiltshire and Gloucestershire, instead of producing food to feed the world are given over to gigantic solar farms? They are a visual blot on the landscape (only second to the hideous wind turbines more or less everywhere); their funding is obscure and, in some cases, corrupt (clever Wall Street funding structures for them will collapse as surely as they did in 2008). Their government subsidy will be paid by all energy consumers in much higher household bills (an estimated £134 pa); and they only work when its relatively sunny. Why can they not be built across Europe, Africa, Asia in return for aid? They've got the sun out there, and all they need is a decent interconnector with the UK, which modern technology looks increasingly likely to be able to provide.

The same applies to the huge surplus of geothermal energy being produced – and largely wasted – in Iceland. Discussions are quite advanced about an Interconnector with Scotland, which would obviate the need for any more wind or solar power. New technology and nuclear power are likely to be long terms more sustainable than the giant Wall Street-funded vanity mirrors of solar farms which stretch across Wiltshire and South West England.

It's a disgrace. Not only all of that, but also how can it be that while Brazil's agricultural prosperity is to a good degree the result of huge investment in farming research, we in Britain are starving our agricultural research organisations of funding? If we are to feed the world, we need to know how to do so in the most productive and imaginative way possible. Dog and stick farming will not achieve it.

Nor will a *Daily Mail* knee-jerk reaction against genetic modification help. Organic, extensive farming has its place. Of course it does. We comfortable middle classes don't mind paying a little extra in the farm shop for free-range eggs. And we are pretty much ready to sign up to the environmental alarmist's vision of animals with two heads as a result of GM.

But science demonstrates that nothing could be further from the truth. We have understood the survival of the fittest since Darwin first explained his theory. We know that if we breed animals, humans and crops in certain ways then the end result will be better. Our healthy, strapping six-foot tall rosy cheeked and long-living Brits today prove it. Breeding and feeding. A glance at my Brazilian farmer's crops in comparison to the poor production throughout most of subsistence farming Africa should be enough to convince you. Undoubtedly we have to use

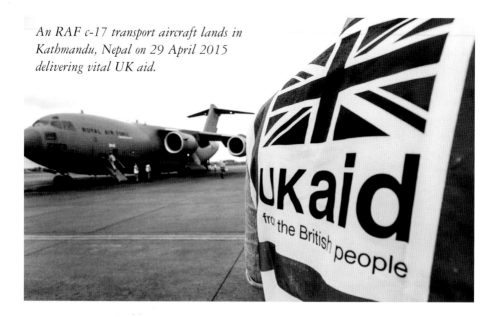

An RAF c-17 transport aircraft lands in Kathmandu, Nepal on 29 April 2015 delivering vital UK aid.

whatever science has to offer to produce the food – and in different ways the water and energy – which the developing world needs. Not to do so is not only inhumane; it is also strategically a grave mistake. We owe it to future generations – across the globe – to feed and water them. That must be our first and primary duty in the century which lies ahead.

So our oft-maligned Overseas Aid spending can easily be justified from a humanitarian, as well as a strategic standpoint. Even if it were not our job as decent human beings to look after the world's poor and starving, it is most firmly in our best interest from a geopolitical perspective. The world would collapse into chaos were it not for continuing and generous aid packages from the wealthy North to the impoverished South. Of all of that there can be little doubt.

But to that paean of Aid-related self-praise must be added some very real caveats. First there can be no doubt that over the decades enormous amounts of aid money has disappeared into the corrupt Swiss bank accounts of Third World dictators. Much aid was at one time paid via national governments, with the obvious consequences of corruption and diversion of the funds from their proper purposes. More recently funds have tended to be sent either direct to particular projects, or via Non-Governmental Organisations. I remember, for example, visiting an outstandingly good school for girls just outside Kathmandu in Nepal. I was proud of the British pounds which were directly going to the better education of these women, who would without doubt make an important contribution to the better government of the country. And it is excellent that direct British aid of this kind is now (thanks to former Aid Minister Sir Alan Duncan) actually branded as 'UKAid'. Is it not astonishing that for years under the last Labour Government we were so embarrassed by our overseas aid projects that it was all done anonymously? It is good nowadays to see huge Union Flag logos all over our aid packages. There must be a direct PR benefit to the UK from it.

Most of the Non-Governmental Organisations do outstandingly good work. Again, there was some concern a few years ago about the percentage of donations being used by the charitable NGOs for central administration. Of the £30 million raised by the BBC Children in Need project in 2006, for example, £3million went to cover the costs of the programmes. Cancer Research that year raised £300 million from public donations, but spent more than £70 million in the process. Similarly, the NSPCC received £90 million but spent £18 million. The top 500 fundraising charities spent on average 9% of their total expenditure on fundraising and publicity that year.

There are 195,289 charities registered in the UK, which collectively raise and spend some £80 billion. Together they employ more than 1 million staff, and make 13 billion 'asks' for money every year – or the equivalent of 200 approaches to each of us. In England and Wales there are 1939 active charities focused on children, 581 charities trying to find a cure for cancer, 354 charities for birds, 255 charities for animals, 81 charities for people with alcohol problems and 69 charities fighting leukaemia. (David Craig: *The Great Charity Scandal*). Amongst overseas aid charities, Oxfam spends £368 million a year; Christian Aid £95 million, ActionAid £49 million, CAFOD £49 million and Care International £39 million. That is without mentioning War on Want, World Vision, Concern Worldwide and Comic Relief.

Oxfam spends £20.3 million annually on campaigns and advocacy (2013/14 annual report). Last year they raised £385.5 million; and of every £10 raised, £6.34 is spent on 'saving lives.' So NGOs are demonstrably better than payments to often corrupt foreign governments or rulers, but some discretion is still needed.

An enormous part of our aid spending has in the past gone via the EU, a yet more questionable way of doing it, since, of course there is no direct national benefit from it. The EU has earmarked $68 billion for aid between 2014 and 2020 (although thankfully we will be well out of it by then.) That's without counting the $32 billion budgeted over the same period by the European Development Fund, the EU's main aid arm, and an average of $9 billion in loans. Of all of that £1.3 billion comes directly from the UK, out of the £12.1 billion we spend over all. Yet the money spent by the EU and EDF is even less accountable than that of the UK, and there have been consistent reports of money being badly mis-spent. Last year, for example, EDF gave £400 million of British cash to fund projects in Robert Mugabe's Zimbabwe and sending officials to the Caribbean to discuss renewable energy. A total of £152,293, according to the *Daily Express* was handed over to projects including trapeze, acrobatics and juggling in Tanzania as part of a 'Fit for Life Scheme.'

Part of the reason for money being used in ways which are best described as questionable must be the absurd decision by the Tory/Lib Dem coalition to write the 0.7% of GDP spending target into law. That is absurd in its own terms. What happens if not enough has been spent? Who scampers around at the end of the financial year to find a few more projects to make up the 0.7%? What if a great deal more is needed through some kind of a global catastrophe. Will we pride ourselves on achieving a false target even if woefully inadequate? Surely we should be spending whatever is necessary to do what is needed in the world according to pre-set reasoning, and according to what is of clear and demonstrable benefit to British people?

There is a constitutional monstrosity here, which also applies to the Child Poverty and Carbon Reduction targets which the previous Labour Government similarly set into law. These are matters for governments to decide on. If they do not do what their electorate wishes, then they will pay the price at the ballot box at the following General Election. By writing them into law there is some kind of a suggestion that if the targets are not achieved, a penalty will be payable. But by whom? Will the Secretary of State go to prison? Of course not. Perhaps we will fine ourselves for their non-achievement, the fines of course being paid back into the Treasury – the very people who were, of course, 'guilty' of that non-achievement.

Writing otherwise perfectly laudable targets into law in this way is self-regarding and foolish.

There should also, I think, be a much weaker barrier between aid spending and spending on defence and the Foreign Office. It must on some occasions be very difficult to discern which budget such spending should come from. Defence activities (for example deploying troops to help in a disaster) should at very least be charged at full value pound for pound against the budget. And if aid spending is in reality simply for diplomatic or defence benefits, then presumably those budgets should take them.

I am also rather of the view that having a separate department – DFID – for Overseas Aid spending is foolish, and to a degree self-congratulatory. I would really much rather see aid programme needs administered alongside normal diplomacy and therefore by the Foreign and Commonwealth Office.

So Britain has a demonstrable altruistic, moral need to provide humanitarian help to those most in need around the world. But we also have a huge strategic benefit to be derived from it if our aid spending is used sensibly, and planned alongside diplomatic and military planning. It can, and it should be, money well spent.

11. Trade, Aid or War?

"Aid and Trade are a lot cheaper than sending soldiers." (Abridged)
(Former US Defence Secretary Robert Gates)

The Perfect Storm I described in Chapter 2 is, of course, assuming the worst. It assumes a global economic collapse, climate change, wars and migrations all happening more or less simultaneously. And it is right to acknowledge that if they did, it would doubtless lead to some kind of apocalyptic implosion, the end product of which is impossible to imagine. What's more, if everything I described in Chapter 2 were to happen and to happen simultaneously, there is in reality precious little that any of us could do to stop it. Just imagine it:

The year is 2025. The Arctic ice has all but disappeared, the oceans are a metre deeper; several Indian Ocean islands have disappeared altogether, Bangladesh is under water, and large parts of Europe and the US are suffering from uncontrollable flooding. Russia controls the Eastern Mediterranean; the EU has collapsed under unprecedented migrant flows and the crisis in the Euro; many parts of the Middle East and Asia Minor are in high kinetic warfare, India and Pakistan threatening nuclear action; President Kim Jong-un has bombed South Korea, China and the US are squaring up over it. The world's economy is in melt-down after the Chinese economic collapse; there is poverty, starvation and thirst throughout the developed world, with civil breakdowns and rioting everywhere as a result. President Trump and Prime Minister Corbyn are in daily contact in the aftermath of the sclerotic incapacity of both NATO and UN.

It may sound a little hyperbolic, but at least some of these elements are perfectly possible, and it is incumbent on all of us to agree what can be done to prevent or ameliorate the effects of each of them. In particular, the purpose of this book is to try to tease out what role the UK should have in doing so.

The first thing to acknowledge is that there is of course a great deal that we can do about at least most of it. Every decision, every action by every nation in the world, by every multinational and supranational organisation (NATO, UN the former, EU the latter) should be designed to address some aspect of one or other of the elements of our Perfect Storm. Free global trade, finally unshackled from the restrictions imposed by membership of the EU has a huge role to play, as does our generous overseas aid programme. Both things bring relief on a global basis.

Governments battle constantly with carbon reduction; the UN and NATO as well as nation states and coalitions of them use military force or deterrence to counter human wickedness and greed wherever it may appear. The EU battles with its economic and structural challenges, the US does what it can to counter Chinese dominance. All of us are engaged in a constant battle against one or more of the influences I have outlined. And with a following wind we may well succeed in lessening their effects or even reversing them. So the storm may turn out, if we are lucky and energetic, to be less perfect (or more imperfect) than we might have feared.

But does all of that myriad action have to be as pragmatic, individualistic as that? Or is there a role for coordination, for grand strategy, for working together in a coordinated way? Surely there must be. But is it supranational? Or multinational? Do humanly created structures placed above coherent and individual government and national structures solve religious, economic and political conflict? Or do they make them worse? Can the United Nations really be a global force for good, or is it an over bloated piece of bureaucratic idealism? What of NATO – an outdated (or in President Trump's subsequently redacted words 'obsolete') military structure to protect us from Soviet Socialism? Or can it be an alliance of the willing against the evils of Islamic Fundamentalism? Can the World Trade Organisation overcome the self-interest of its individual members in favour of mutually helpful global free trade?

Or are artificial human constructs of this kind doomed to failure before they start? Are the genes of catastrophe inbuilt into their construction? Or is multi-nationalism – countries voluntarily doing things together on a bilateral or multi-lateral basis not more likely to succeed since it garners rather than tries to suppress self-interest?

With the exception a few brilliant minds and statesmen-like leaders, world history is rarely driven by long-term planning, or even much by human intent. For even those brilliant leaders and armchair generals may sometimes be wise only after the event. Churchill is well known to have suffered from *'esprit d'escalier'* – thoughts on the staircase. 'That's what I ought to have said", quickly becomes in a subsequent anecdote 'Here's what I said then.' History is not written by planners (as Stalin proves), but by what that great statesman Harold Macmillan described as *"Events, dear boy, events."*

Britain has a vast amount to offer the world, and perhaps a better cross-blend of things than any other single nation.

After Brexit, we will be better able to flex our military and diplomatic muscles through alliances and organisations – NATO, the UN, even the European Security and Defence Initiative. We can be the reliable partner in a series of coalitions of the willing, spreading free market liberal democracy around the world – something of the NeoCon agenda.

The second great challenge facing us all is our globe itself and what we want to do with it. We all recognise that resources are limited. If we are not very careful we will run out of food and water. But we will also run out of energy, including petrol without which our world would not currently operate; we will run out of living space if we do not do something about our planning system and the magnetic effect which our great cities have on people. Cities are becoming bigger and bigger and less and less sustainable, while large parts of our countryside are being progressively depopulated.

Russia, for example, is the greatest landmass in the world. The country's 17.09 million square kilometres cover one eighth of the world's inhabited area, 4200 miles from Kaliningrad in the west to Vladivostock and Magadan in the Far East, and about 2800 miles from north to south. The Russian border is the longest in the world at 35,910 miles. Yet the population of 146 million is almost wholly based in a very few cities (Moscow: 13 million, St Petersburg: 5 million, then about 13 others with a population of one million or more, and a further 150 cities ranging from 1 million down to 100,000. In other words, probably half of Russia's population lives in 100 or so towns and cities, nearly all of them to the east of the Urals. Siberia alone covers 13.1 million square kilometres, or 77% of Russia's land area; it is twice the size of France, yet it has a total population of 800,000.

It took me eight hours recently to fly from Moscow to Magadan, during which we passed over few if any habitations far less towns or cities.

Magadan is the grim city – closed until recently – through which passed so many of the 30 million or so political prisoners destined for the Gulag. One million of them died building the 'Road of Bones' along which we drove. It is only passable in deep winter when the roads are frozen. In summer they become a muddy and impassable swamp in places, infested by mosquitoes vicious enough to kill a man (one of the agonising methods of execution in the Gulag.) We visited several of the old prisons, many now converted into (pretty basic) blocks of grim flats, some still inhabited by the original prisoners or their descendants, trapped in Siberia by their poor pay in the local gold and diamond mines barely equalling a single flight to Moscow.

One old grey-bearded ex-prisoner we met in the middle of nowhere confided that he had escaped from the Gulag many years ago, and had lived largely off mare's milk in a log hut ever since. I enquired if he had been lonely. "Oh no," he confided. "I got a lovely wife from the Philippines on the Internet. Big breasts...." Imagine her disappointment at meeting the oligarch she had expected from the Internet advert – an old escaped prisoner 1000 miles from the nearest habitation.

But aside from that old friend, and a mosque whose golden crescent suddenly loomed up from the deep snow around a deserted prison serving the Chechnya Moslems similarly exiled in the area, and the small population of Chakutka natives, we met almost nobody for 2000 miles. We drove to the 'Pole of Cold', Oymakon, where the temperature was minus 52 degrees Celcius on the day we were there (the record is minus 72 Celcius). The cold stopped us breathing easily and allowed the old experiment of chucking a bucket of hot water in the air and watching it form a frozen waterfall before it hit the ground. (Why does it not work with a bucket of cold water?)

The fact is that a very large part of Russia (especially since the collapse of the USSR) is unpopulated. Male life expectancy now stands at sixty-four years of age,

with a quarter of all males not reaching the age of fifty-five. The ratio of men to women is 1 to 10. They are desperately setting up fertility clinics to try to INCREASE the birth rate, while much of the rest of the world is struggling to do exactly the opposite.

One question we reasonably have to ask is "Is there a limit to growth?" Are our economists right when they predicate 'success' on 'growth'? May there come a time when economies are stable, and ways of life unchanging generation to generation. Or do we need to create some such thing if we are to stabilise the globe for future generations?

And all of that is without thinking about Global Warming, climate change and the rest of it. The late Michel Rocard, the former French Prime Minister and then French Ambassador to the Polar Regions, once confided to me that if the Greenland ice-caps were to melt, then water levels would increase by 10 meters which would be quite enough to drown two billion people, including a large part of Europe. Even setting aside such extreme Armageddon visions, there can be no doubt that we have to do something about it. The environmental challenge, of course, is also closely linked to the world poverty and starvation challenge. What happens in our environment – the way we use and share our scarce global resources – can have a dramatic effect, for good or ill, on the poor and starving of the world.

Our whole way of life is unhealthy. More and more of us are huddled together in ever-decreasingly sustainable cities and towns leaving vast swathes of the globe wholly unpopulated. I flew eight hours across Siberia to Magadan, and then drove 2000 kilometers to Yakutsk seeing fewer than 500 houses. Yet Moscow, Paris, London and Mexico City are ever increasing vast sprawling industrial, urban nightmares of a place to live. The internal combustion engine has a lot to answer for – both in terms of pollution and accelerating usage of our ever-scarcer resources; but also for hastening our way and speed of life without any noticeable improvement in the quality of it. Our countryside is a largely ignored (leaving aside the chocolate box) commodity. "Oh, to be in England now that April's there" quoth Robert Browning. Not "Oh to be in Manchester, Leeds, Glasgow or Cardiff." It's the green fields, the forests, moors, heath and highland we yearn for. But how few of us find time in our mad car-enabled lives to go there for any bar the most passing of visits? We Westerners are crammed together in our unhealthy, energy sapping, mind numbing city agglomerations getting fat and idle and foolish as a result.

Malthus, writing around 1780 would have been wholly familiar with the exponential growth in population compared to the arithmetic growth in food supply leading to starvation, poverty and civil disobedience, perhaps even migration and warfare.

What a contrast with the East. Their vast intellectual ability and general entrepreneurial energy is only now beginning to emerge. They have also discovered wheat as opposed to rice, and are rapidly developing a taste for beef and dairy products. There are huge implications in that for the way we as a world produce our food.

Wake up! Is I think my message. The world is changing at a rate none of us can comprehend. It is exponential and plus some. I do not wholly subscribe to the Limits to Growth agenda. Nor do I necessarily believe the worst predictions of the environmental disaster gloom mongers, although I do rather like a gently precautionary principle approach to the whole thing. But what is certain is that patterns of growth and consumption (and therefore production, at least of energy and foodstuffs) throughout most of the world is changing at a mind-blowing rate. We in Britain can either be part of that dazzling revolution – help it along, guide it in the right direction, monitor its progress, and indeed profit from recognising the skills and abilities which it needs; or we can be left behind in our over-consuming obsolete, fat and idle ways.

There is another – less discussed – cycle here. It's the growth – healthy riches – bloated profligacy – collapse – austerity – phoenix-like rebirth cycle. It happens in every age, every part of the world. It happens in one form or another in most human activities. It happened to the Roman and British Empires; it happens in economies (despite Gordon Brown's vainglorious claim to have 'ended boom and bust'); it happens in our everyday lives (New Year's resolutions following the Christmas splurge).

It may be my Scots Presbyterianism showing through, but my guess is that we in the West are pretty bloated right now. We eat and drink and consume to our hearts content whether or not we can afford it financially or environmentally. We are overfed, drunken, idle, low-life profligates, and a bit of a culture shock would do us all very little harm.

A bit of a culture shock – a limit to growth, a degree of concern for the poor and starving people of the world; a bit of belt tightening to try to avoid the worst climate cataclysms predicted would do us all no harm at all. It might also be a step towards avoiding some of the political and military consequences which may well be just as real as the more often discussed environmental ones.

The environment and poverty are also central to the third great challenge facing us in the twenty-first century – religion. It was religion, of course, which dominated national and international life for the best part of the last millennium. The Crusades, Reformation and Revolution, the religious wars of the seventeenth and eighteenth centuries, even as recently as The Troubles in Northern Ireland and ethnic conflict in the Balkans were all curious amalgams of poverty, lust, greed, aggression all under the convenient camouflage of religious conviction. Yet while we all hope that pious warfare may well be a thing of history here in the civilised West, it most certainly is not throughout much of the rest of the world.

By far the most obvious and most worrying example, of course, is fundamentalist jihadist Islam. But we should never forget Sunni versus Shia; Jew versus Palestinian; Iranian versus Saudi etc etc. The reality is that global peace and security is as much threatened by misplaced religious convictions today as it was for most of the last 100 years.

So we may be facing a Perfect Storm. The world may be teetering on the edge of disaster. But there is a huge amount that we in post-Brexit Britain can do about it. There are things which can be of huge benefit to the world, and perhaps almost coincidentally of huge benefit to the UK. And many of them are contributions or actions which have been inhibited or prevented, or subsumed by our membership of the EU.

Trade must be the greatest, humanitarian aid somewhere close behind it. Military strength is essential, at very least from a deterrence standpoint. But so are contributions like: our constitution, Parliamentary democracy and legal and judicial systems; our diplomatic abilities, our Universities, science and think tanks, our farming and environmental practices on which we can lead the threatened world; and so much more. Let us have a look at each of them in turn.

12. Britain: A Diplomatic Power

"Speak softly and Carry a big stick." (President Teddy Roosevelt)

It is pretty widely perceived (and pretty accurately, I think) that it was the Foreign and Commonwealth Office, who, having lost the empire, instead drove Britain into the European Union. It then became infamous for its ability to make a Euro-federalist out of the staunchest British Eurosceptic.

There is some irony that the FCO is now the institution, under Boris Johnson's guiding hand, which has overall responsibility (alongside David Davis's Department for Brexit) for leading Britain out of the EU and into the wider world, as a newly independent nation state. To do so, and in line with the people's clearly expressed wish in the Referendum, there will have to be a wholly new approach to diplomacy, security, soft power and trade. That must be driven by the fundamental belief that Britain is newly open to the world, and a determination to re-engage with the globe in a way the Foreign Office has not really done for forty-five years. That will without doubt be a challenge for the overwhelmingly pro-EU FCO mandarins. But the end product may be just what is needed to reinvigorate and re-empower the Foreign Office itself as an institution of power and influence in the world.

The foreign and commonwealth Office.

For perhaps the most exciting aspect of Britain's future outside the European Union lies in its foreign policy, despite the critics who crow that the vote to leave was a vote for Britain to turn in on itself and withdraw from the world. The opposite must of course be the case – that for Britain to thrive beyond the realms of the EU we must embrace the world in all its opportunity.

The *Financial Times'* style guide during the 2016 referendum, perhaps unsurprisingly, recommended against using the word 'Brexiteer'. As Michael Gove remarked, the term conjured up *"buccaneer, pioneer, musketeer. It lends a sense of panache and romance to the argument."* It is vaguely reminiscent of Sir Francis Drake, and other seaborne heroes of British history and it could not be further from the dry as dust Europhiles. The 'Brexiteer' is a globe-trotting character, with eyes far beyond continental Europe. Above all the Brexiteer is an optimist, and an opportunist. The committed Euro-loving *FT* hated the Brexiteers' image of Brexit as being an unashamedly exciting proposition.

Britain is a fundamentally 'global' nation, one of the most global of them all. An early election slogan for the Leave Campaign was "Go Global", (although whether that would have won the Referendum in place of the eventual slogan, "Vote Leave, Take Control" is debatable.) It is undeniable that the vote to leave the European Union was the cry of a nation aching to reclaim its rank as an independent, free trading, outward- and forward-looking country, rather than any desire to pull up drawbridges and contract out horizons.

Britain joined the Common Market in 1972 under a shadow of decline, with waning imperial pretensions, and insecurity on the world stage. The Foreign Office, once the world's intellectual and foreign affairs cockpit in the nineteenth century had been shaken by the gross humiliation of the Suez Crisis, and our withdrawal from east of Suez, which seemed to affirm Britain's newfound smallness in the world.

"Great Britain has lost an empire, but has not yet found a role."

(Dean Acheson, Harry Truman's Secretary of State, 1962.)

The Foreign Office hoped that membership of the EU would provide it with a reinvigorated role. Yet in many ways, political union within the EU robbed the Foreign Office of a huge amount of its purpose. Over forty years, the EU grew into the fabric of British politics and law, and had such an impact on domestic policy, that it ceased to be primarily a Foreign Office concern.

It may therefore ironically be the case that once we are freed of political union, we will find our interest in European affairs increasing, rather than declining. The Foreign Office will then have to engage properly with the EU as an allied power, and indeed an incredibly powerful neighbour. Rather than sending MEPs to Brussels to contribute to a powerless European Parliament, we must learn to reengage with the capitals of Europe, and the nations of the great continent, in which we will continue to play a significant and influential role.

No longer will we have commissioners and bureaucrats bouncing back and forth between Brussels and Strasbourg, keeping up to date with federalist gossip and supranational plotting over lunch. Britain, and the Foreign Office, will need to rediscover its European partners, redistribute its diplomats from Brussels to the capitals, gain the ear of national governments, and revive its once famous ability to influence European affairs from across the Channel.

That will not be an easy task. Unravelling forty years of British and European integration will be hard enough, but then engaging in a positive way with the remaining 27 nations who will remain members of a determinedly supranational EU will be a very real challenge. It is an intellectual challenge which will no doubt once again attract some of the very best of civil service brains.

There are rich prospects for diplomacy and for the Foreign Office itself. It should once again become an intellectual power house knowing more about every nation on the globe than it does itself. Central to that is intelligence, political analysis, military power, soft power including overseas aid, trade in all of its forms, control of visas and immigration, and even consular services for British nationals living overseas. Many of those tools of diplomacy are for now at least the prerogative of other government departments – Brexit, Overseas Trade, and International Aid, as well as Immigration and Nationality all have their own Secretaries of State and departments independent of the Foreign Office. Yet in a very real sense the Foreign Office should be the spider at the heart of all of their webs, to ensure that we use every instrument in the orchestra for the betterment of Britain's interests overseas.

The Diplomatic Service should first of all have at its command the best intelligence and shrewdest analysis of political developments on the ground across the world. Aided of course by the three main British intelligence agencies, MI5, MI6 and GCHQ, and by the rest of the UK secret intelligence community, who have generally preserved their global pre-eminence, the Foreign Office itself must have the most sophisticated and capable intelligence analysis machinery in the world. For that it must command the best brains and the smartest technology. But it must also reinvent its spirit of outstanding excellence in global political intelligence and analysis, and in historical analysis, which it seems rather to have lost with recent rather self-regardingly meritocratic reforms.

The UK has always stood tall in the world. We are members of the G7; a permanent member of the UN Security Council; Europe's most senior, willing, and high spending member of NATO; an independent nuclear power; and a member of the Five Eyes. (Five Eyes is the pre-eminent international intelligence sharing partnership amongst the UK, USA, Canada, Australia, and New Zealand which predates the European Union. It has, for example, had a crucial role to play in the worldwide war on terror.)

There is a very good reason why the five permanent members of the UN Security Council are who they are: nuclear weapons, and powerful, sophisticated armed forces. Put simply, strength buys influence. Clausewitz's famous nostrum that "Diplomacy without arms is like an orchestra without instruments", demands that Britain should remain an eminent military power, with advanced, highly capable armed forces, which can be mobilised across the globe faster than any other nation, second only to the United States.

Yet, as we saw in a previous chapter, our continuing military – and therefore diplomatic – strength demands a fundamental re-examination of our capabilities, and especially our commitment to defence spending. If we are truly to speak softly, but wield a big stick, then we had better make sure that we grow some pretty hefty knobkerries and shillelagh.

Traditional intelligence and diplomacy and military strength are of course of themselves unimportant if they are not deployed for the better safety, economic security and trading capabilities of our citizens. Our EU and extra-EU trade is an essential 'must' in the post-Brexit world.

The EU's Common External Tariff had long-since trapped the United Kingdom within the confines of the European market. For a nation which owes its historic wealth to global trade and exploration having our trade policy bound and limited by the European Union felt uncomfortably protectionist. Once the leading free trading nation, Britain became bound by a continental tariff, unable to import at will, shorn of its traditional trading partnerships with Australia and New Zealand, all seemingly to pander to the protectionist instincts of the French farming lobby. It is hard to underestimate the resentment this caused: the import duties paid on second-hand electronics bought online from America, the African agricultural economy starved of growth by Europe's barriers, and the perverse, wasteful incentives created by the Common Agricultural Policy.

Yet reviving our global trading ambitions, which must be one of the most central themes of Brexit should not make us into some kind of neo-Elizabethan mercantilist nation ruthlessly pursuing profit above all else. We will be open for business, but it would be foolish, and incredibly damaging, for Britain to disregard the domestic character and sensitivities of its allies and trading partners.

All nations have debts and obligations, and it is imperative that British diplomacy in the age of Brexit recognises this. Britain is complicit in creating the conditions which led to our vote to leave in 2016. We were, for example, instrumental in expanding the European Union eastwards which may, with hindsight, have been a mistake, resulting in the unprecedented waves of eastern European migration to our shores which was of itself one of the drivers for Brexit.

The understanding of debt and obligations will also be important to trade deals. Whilst trade between individuals is fundamentally transactional, between nations and continents it takes on another character. It is political, it is emotional, and it is even irrational. Economic self-interest sometimes has to take second place to vital political and diplomatic priorities. With worldwide tariff barriers at historic lows, trade agreements are tussles over far thornier issues today: harmonisation of standards, professional services, and increasingly immigration.

At once essential and incendiary, an economic asset, as well as political poison, immigration was seen by many as a keen driver of Brexit. Traditionally an issue for the Home Office, it will grow steadily relevant to the Foreign Office in our post-EU future.

For the very nature of trade agreements is changing. British diplomats may well find themselves in the future haggling over visas in their efforts to open up new markets for British exports. India's blunt insistence on more flexible immigration rules, particularly for students wishing to come to Britain, may well be a fore-runner of other international trading negotiations to come. Britain must realise what the world wants from us. Yes, it may well be Scotch whisky, specialist engineering and cars; but it is also access to our jobs market, courses in British universities, and – controversially to many – contracts in our health service.

Mobile labour is an unavoidable reality in the twenty-first century. We enjoy historically low unemployment and a growing economy: so of course migration is required to maintain a healthy economy. The world has grown ever smaller, and departing the EU, with its discriminatory migration rules, now gives us the freedom to seek out the finest talent anywhere in the world. That, of course is in complete contradistinction to the current open door policy within the EU, under which all 750 million Europeans have a perfect right to come to the UK to live and work. And it must also put a real brake on any threat of the kind of mass migration we discussed in a previous chapter. Britain must be open and welcoming to the world without the current net immigration of over 300,000 people per year.

The British Council and our network of embassies around the world advertise Britain to the globe, and shout about the opportunities that lie in our land, and it is no wonder that Britain is the final destination for so many of the world's jobseekers. Yet we should consider how we can also use our embassies and trade missions to help improve employment prospects overseas by spreading the conditions for growth and prosperity as widely as we can. Britain has long attracted the best and brightest, but with, for example, the World Health Organisation estimating that there is a global shortage of two million healthcare professionals, it is surely right and proper that we should prioritise training British doctors and nurses at home, rather than draining the developing world of such essential workers as we currently do.

It is worth, as an example, pondering the reasons behind the declining number of Polish migrants to the UK in the last couple of years. Rather than being the result of a rising tide of post-referendum xenophobia, as many hysterically claimed, the reality is far simpler. Poland's economy is booming. One of the few nations not to experience recession in 2008, the possessor of an independent and healthy currency, and predicted economic growth of over 3 per cent in 2017, it is no wonder the Polish Diaspora is returning home.

Just as an independent Britain should use its regained seat at the WTO to become a world-leader in promoting open and liberal economies, so should its diplomats and ambassadors attempt to influence the world for the better with international aid. Our focus should be far broader than crisis relief, and instead explore how to expand democracy, engineer economic growth, and improve education around the world.

To make the idea of Global Britain a reality, we must be a leading voice for free and fair international trade, and defend to the hilt at the World Trade Organisation the rules we forged in the past. The Western world – the leaders in free trade – is turning against open markets and liberal economics. President Trump proudly sees prosperity in protectionism, whilst European and American voters alike have emphatically rejected the idea of increased international trade, perhaps bringing to a halt many successful years of market liberalisation and economic development.

No longer a fiercely liberal counterweight to the power-based economic games of China, the West is retreating, insulating defensive domestic industries, and closing itself from the world. When the European Union maintains the Common Agricultural Policy, France's supposedly liberal President Macron suggests a 'buy European' policy, and the United States government attempts to punish American firms for outsourcing, we must ensure that Britain continues to lead the world as an open, free, and welcoming economy, unafraid of the world, and excited by its opportunity. Britain owes its current wealth not merely to forty years of European Union membership, but forty years of openness, competitiveness and economic liberalism. With an independent seat at the World Trade Organisation reclaimed, we will have a new platform from which to champion these ideals.

Once independent of the European Union, of course, an ambitious trade policy should be central to all government endeavours, and be a great concern for the Foreign Office. Trade negotiations require diplomatic guile, a deep understanding of other nations, and a coherent geopolitical ambition. All of these traits should be in abundance at the Foreign Office. We must seek – as Acheson said – a role in the world which is not beneficial to Britain alone, but to the world as a whole.

Soft power, the British ideal, the English language, developmental aid, and of course trade must go hand in hand when we design a foreign policy for the future. Whilst many campaigning for Britain to leave the EU also support a drastic reduction – or repurposing of – the foreign aid budget, I believe this would be a mistake. The foreign aid budget has been poorly spent in the past, but it is of great to use to Britain and the world, and as I have said before, something of which I think this country can be proud. Hand in hand with the expansion of trade, foreign aid bolsters our international reputation immeasurably. Like it or not, this reputation will need careful maintenance in the future. It is undeniable that leaving the European Union has tarnished, and perhaps even soured, formerly friendly international relationships. It will be important to stay ahead of the curve and shape the narrative ourselves, before one is thrust upon us. Britain is not a nation in decline; she is not a nation hiding from the world; Britain has not abandoned her obligations. An enthusiastic, and ambitious commitment to foreign aid will go a long way in ensuring this will not be the case. Good will is a valuable currency, and as Britain ventures into independence, she can not have too much of it.

Few institutions are better at projecting Britain to the world than the BBC World Service. Hand in hand with the Foreign Office, the World Service must become Britain's voice once again, the leading source of news the world over, reinvigorated and expanded as a proud symbol of Britain's continued interest in the world at large. We live in an era of increasingly cavalier, partisan and pernicious news. Kremlin-backed RT (formerly Russia Today) continues to push an insidious Putinist line around the world, proudly playing fast-and-loose with the truth in Europe as it exploits weaknesses and division in the EU. Qatar's Al-Jazeera news network has leapt ahead of the BBC World Service for popularity in the region, and was instrumental in raising Qatar's reputation in the world, transforming its capital Doha into a Geneva-on-the-Gulf, where Middle East peace deals were brokered. Yet following the Arab Spring, Al-Jazeera threw itself behind Islamist terror, and trashed Qatar's reputation accordingly. Whilst insurgent news networks in the West attract new, disenchanted audiences who look up the 'mainstream media' with contempt, the developing world is a territory ripe for the BBC World Service's expansion. Just look at the dominance of France24 in Francophone Africa: such a powerful media force throughout Africa, it is followed as the authoritative news source in the region, and it inevitably associates France with objectivity, truth, and informative reporting. The continued development of the World Service would prove one of the most important tools of soft power in our arsenal. It will ensure Britain is visible from every corner of the globe, and that the whole world is in London's reach. In 2017, the BBC launched a new wave of services abroad, reaching viewers in Nigeria, Kenya, Ethiopia, India, the Arab world, Russia, and even North Korea. Media freedom is being curtailed around the world, and the BBC World Service is not simply an instrument of truth and quality journalism, it is a counterweight to the state-sponsored broadcasting of Russia and China, and is a beacon of Western, democratic values. Such an asset cannot go un-used; as we re-engage with the world beyond Europe on our own terms, we must use the World Service at every turn. Not as an instrument of colonialism or manipulation, but as a bridge across the world.

Another crown jewel of British soft power is the British Council. A cultural institution from the 1930s, the Council is far more than a colonial relic. It is an educational powerhouse, which has brought the English language, high quality English education and British culture to over one hundred countries across the world. Its very foundation is something of which we can be proud: in 1934, it was established by the Foreign Office as a cultural and educational institution to fight the rise of fascism across the globe. If we are to agree that soft power in the age of Brexit will be vital, then we must not preside over the diminishment of the British Council. Indeed, in such a turbulent world, we must reinvigorate the Council with its original purpose, to inculcate the world against tyranny. Few efforts could do more to prevent post-Brexit Britain being defined by its critics and its sceptics. The Council's charter dates from 1940. It states that the Council's intention is to use Britain's cultural resources to promote the interchange of knowledge, ideas, and discovery, to build knowledge, friendship, and understand between the people of the world. A full-throated cry of these noble principles is required. Britain is no parochial nation, and Brexit was no parochial move, but indeed the complete opposite.

The Foreign Office could hardly have more tools at its disposal. As well as the cultural powerhouse that is the British Council, and the important work done by the Department for International Development, we have a huge network of embassies, high commissions and consulates. In the years running up to the Referendum, it was a point of pride that Britain was opening more embassies around the world, and taking its diplomatic mission to broader horizons. William Hague oversaw this excellent growth in embassies during his time as Foreign Secretary, and I am encouraged that his ambition and scope still seems alive in the Foreign Office, and nurtured by ministers who recognise the chance to engage with the world without having to go through the prism of Brussels. Africa is surely the engine of the future, and with our network of 36 embassies and high commissions, 19 British Council, and 16 DFID offices over Africa, we have the opportunity to contribute to this growth, and become the continent's leading international partner. As the largest European investor in sub-Saharan Africa, we must reinvigorate and renew our relations with the great continent after our liberation from the EU.

It was popularly imagined in the early twentieth century that the future of diplomacy was increasingly continental, with little place for independent nations. Brexit is a chance for Britain to prove this assumption wholly wrong. That can only be done with a rejuvenated diplomacy and a rigorously internationalist approach to the world. Our democracy must allow it, of course, but Brexit need not be a parochial move, which sees Britain retreat from the world. Nor should it see us attempt to revive an imperial nostalgia, which will leave a sour taste in the mouth of many at home and abroad. Diplomacy after Brexit must strive to be a force for good in the world: a driver of prosperity and economic reform, political freedom, and peace. We must not forget the considerable tools we have to hand. An unrivalled ambassadorial infrastructure; a proud and leading commitment to developmental aid; the sort of cultural soft power most nations can only dream of; and, the military capability – and willingness to use it – to bolster our standing in the world. There can be no doubt that this will be a challenge. Britain is choosing the open sea once again, and I believe she shall find prosperity over the waves once again.

13. Britain: A Military Power

"Arma Pacis Fulcra."
("Arms are the Balance of Peace.")
(Motto of Honourable Artillery Company)

There are those who welcome the end of our involvement in overseas wars as an end to 'interventionism' in the world. There are those who support cuts in defence spending as a diversion of scarce resources to the Home Front. There are those who attack Overseas Aid spending, arguing, amongst other things, and slightly oddly, that it is money which would be better spent on the Somerset Levels. There are those who are opposed to warfare of any kind, and some who would leave the peace of the world to America or 'someone else'.

There is some intellectual strength in each of those arguments. Yet if any of them was to hold sway, it would imply a very significant change in Britain's global influence. Is our membership of the UN Security Council and of NATO important to us? Do we have any residual moral obligation to play our part in securing international peace and security? Or does our defence outlook end at Calais with an isolationist abandonment of our global duties?

The 2015 Strategic Defence and Security Review (SDSR) lays out a 'hierarchy' of military risks for which we must prepare ourselves. At least that part of it seems a fairly sketchy, and apparently ill-thought-through document. Its authors gave evidence to the Commons Defence Select Committee and got themselves in a pretty awful muddle trying to defend the pretty arbitrary choices they had made for 'High,' 'Medium,' or 'Low'. For example, "Instability Overseas" had been a Tier 2 risk in SDSR 2010, but got promoted to Tier 1 in 2015, while "attacks and pressures on allies" is apparently a Tier 2 risk, and "a military attack on the UK, Overseas Territories or bases is considered a Tier 3 risk (or extremely unlikely.) We shall see...

It's a pretty tenuous list, since as every armchair general knows, all you can expect in warfare is the unexpected. (And yes, we know, generals always fight the previous war; and the best laid plans never survive first contact with the enemy.) It may be instructive that the previous SDSR, in 2010 failed to predict the Arab Spring; it had never heard of Daesh/ISIS; it did not yet know that David Cameron was planning to pull out of Afghanistan; and it foresaw no risk of a resurgent Russia. Good planning, eh?

Every war and military engagement of recent times has come out of the blue – the Argentinian invasion of the Falklands shortly after we had withdrawn our patrol vessels; Saddam's invasion of Kuwait; 9/11 and the consequent invasion of

Iraq and Afghanistan. These and a hundred others were wholly unpredicted by any of the clever people preparing our SDSRs or our military long-term planning. So all you can do is to try to expect the unexpected, keep our military capabilities as flexible as is possible to be ready for anything.

That doctrine of flexible deployability will be decried by two groups of defence thinkers, both of whom could reasonably be accused of "talking their own book." The old school lot would tell you that military action is pointless unless you control ground, and that therefore wholly conventional war-fighting assets are the baseload we need. They decry every battalion that is abolished or amalgamated, argue for main battle tanks, despite the infinitely superior Apache helicopter which does much the same job, except arguably rather better. They hanker after an Army, and to a lesser degree a Navy and Air Force of the '60s or '70s – manpower and equipment heavy.

At the other end of the spectrum there are plenty of clever people who will tell you that all of that is history. We are just too small a nation to go around invading other people. We don't have the manpower (82,000 soldiers in the regular army is the smallest since Waterloo), or the equipment (our Challenger 2 tanks are in a woeful state of disuse and ill-repair), and that anyhow we simply cannot compete with the military might either of our greatest ally the US, or indeed of any of the great forces in the world – China, India and Pakistan, even setting on one side for the moment their nuclear capabilities. Our contribution to coalition efforts, they would argue, should be specialist. Special Forces is one area in which we still excel (although the US are quickly catching up on our blindside, inspired to a degree by joint training with SAS, SBS and SRU); ISTAR (Intelligence, Surveillance, Target Acquisition and Reconnaissance); human and electronic intelligence gathering; counter-IED (roadside bombs) and surveillance, Remotely Piloted Air Systems (drones to you and me), and myriad other specialist military capabilities of that kind. They would maintain that we should be the 'clever' end of war-fighting, supplying our 'heavier' allies like the US with assets of which they are short. And it is perfectly true that despite our comparatively small size, we do make a disproportionate contribution to aerial surveillance and target acquisition for example in the battle against Daesh in Iraq and Syria.

Both schools of thought are of course myopic. Given the sheer unpredictability of world events, limiting ourselves either to conventional warfare (which we can ill-afford), or indeed high tech modern warfare which might well not fit the bill under certain military and strategic circumstances, are almost equally wrong. Flexibility – the ability to fulfil both ends of that spectrum, and a good few more between left and right of arc – must be the watchword. The public would never forgive our politicians if they admitted that they were unprepared for, or unable to deal with, some threat to their wellbeing or livelihoods or the safety of our nation. "The Defence of the Realm is the first duty of Government" they would argue, and they would assuredly heavily punish any government or political party who had forgotten that in some national or international crisis.

So what are those military risks? And what use could better be made of our military assets 'to make the world a better place', or to Make Britain Great again. Leaving aside the lopsided risk hierarchy in the SDSR, there is a range of (reasonably obvious) risks or tasks for our military on land, at sea and in the air.

We must defend our home shores against any kind of aggressor or invader. There is, of course, very little, if any, realistic risk of some foreign state's forces storming up the beach at Dover or dropping their paratroops into our countryside. There really is no imaginable circumstance under which we would have to defend ourselves, at least in these islands, against an aggressive invader.

Yet let's not forget how often the Russians have tested our readiness on several occasions in recent years both by submarine incursion taking advantage of our very foolish lack of any kind of Maritime Patrol Aircraft (a mistake in the 2010 SDSR, rather belatedly corrected in the 2015 version), and by fairly regular overflights by their Tupolev bombers. Russia has once again started its series of 'Zapad' (Russian for 'The West') exercises deploying vast numbers of troops and vehicles just a few hundred miles away from NATO's Baltic states' borders. It is alleged (albeit denied by the Russians) that Zapad 16 culminated in a simulated nuclear strike against Warsaw. And it is for sure that they deploy their 'tactical' nuclear weapons as a routine part of the Zapad exercises. (NATO does not recognise 'tactical' nuclear weapons, arguing that any use of them would be 'strategic.') The vast scale of the exercises should quite rightly send a shiver down the collective spines of NATO. 100,000 heavily armed Russian troops exercise 100 miles or less away from the 750 British troops at battalion level we have deployed in Estonia. (In total NATO strength in the Baltics is about 4/5000). Historically, exercises such as this have been used as cover for an identical aggressive invasion force to follow. Russian forces could cruise more or less uninterrupted at least to the Baltic Sea. A less apocalyptic interpretation might well be that they are leaving large numbers of troops and equipment in Belarus, for example. Alternatively they may be attempting, to reinforce the two divisions of Arctic trained troops near Murmansk a few miles away from the wholly unprotected Norwegian border at Kirkenes. The British government have recently announced that they plan to reduce the outstandingly good Royal Marine cold-weather warfare training in Arctic Norway – just at precisely the same moment as the Russians are building up their Arctic and mountain warfare capabilities. We will come to regret it.

No-one would suggest any remote likelihood of Russia trying to invade the UK in anything like the foreseeable future. But is it not nonetheless right that we should both defend our shores against them, and be seen to be doing so? Conventional deterrence is almost as important as nuclear, especially when dealing with a nation showing real aggressive intent to towards parts of NATO and the EU – namely the three Baltic States, Lithuania, Latvia and Estonia.

Latvia in particular has a significant number of Russian speakers a large part of whom are 'stateless', and without any kind of passport. It would not take much for Russia to argue that they are in some way liberating their own people by an aggressive invasion of Latvia. That, after all, is what they did in the Crimea, and to a degree how they justified their invasion of Eastern Ukraine. An additional incentive in Lithuania, or even Poland would be to secure access to their encircled enclave of Kaliningrad on the Baltic Sea. It is said to be one of the most highly militarised and armed areas in the world, and is of crucial strategic interest to Russia. But at least in theory it is only accessible by air and sea, and with the goodwill of the Lithuanian government.

The difference between Lithuania and Crimea, however, is that the Baltic states are members of NATO (and of the EU), which makers an aggressive land-based invasion a great deal less likely, or at least a great deal more high-risk from Mr Putin's standpoint. More worrying in many ways would be an unconventional attack on the Baltic states which might or might not trigger off an 'Article 5 moment'. If Russia were to broadcast vast quantities of propaganda (which they already do); or if they were to block the airwaves and Internet (as they did against Lithuania in 2007), or if they were to take part in any other form of aggressive cyber warfare, would that be covered under Article 5, which stipulates a collective response to 'armed' aggression? Would the bringing down of the Lithuanian banking system by cyber-means really justify a NATO response? And even if it did would the people of Britain, for example, really be ready for British troops to lose their lives in defence of the Lithuanian banking system? Perhaps not.

Even less 'attributable' would be incursions by the 'men in green uniforms' which were the advanced guard in Ukraine. They wore no marks of identity, nor nationhood; they had no badges of rank. They were anonymous armed men, acting clearly in the interests of their Russian backers but without much risk of real retribution because of their 'deniable' nature. Again, would the British body politic really be ready to support military deployment to Latvia against anonymous groups of armed men in a wood somewhere near the border? I doubt it.

There may well be a strong argument that in this cyber unattributable, asymmetric, terrorist-driven world, Article 5 of the NATO Treaty needs to be amended, especially to delete the reference to 'Armed' aggression. These days it would be perfectly possible to disable a nation such as the UK without a shot having been fired in anger. A major cyber attack on our military, our banking system, or perhaps on our infrastructure like the water system or power providers would be just as catastrophic as Nazi paratroopers landing in Central London. Or by redefining Article 5, are you perhaps making it easier for a potential aggressor to test the outer limits of acceptable behaviour in the knowledge that it will not – quite – trigger an Article 5 moment?

It is of crucial importance that the members of NATO should all hang together against aggression, of whatever type that aggression might take. If not we would assuredly 'all hang separately.'

State on state aggression against British dependencies is, in a way, far more likely. Is it really impossible to imagine renewed Argentinian aggression against the Falklands, for example? What would we do if Gibraltar was attacked, or some of the other lesser UK dependencies? Do we really have the military capability to mount an operation similar to that in the Falklands in 1982? I think not.

We must also be ready to defend our shores – perhaps especially post-Brexit – against illegal immigrants and terrorists who have already shown their determination and ingenuity. The border with Eire will remain open; but so will our massive shoreline, which could not be wholly protected against small boats and aircraft even if we wanted to do so. What's more, the HGV traffic through the port of Dover alone makes total security well-nigh impossible. Dover handled 2.6million freight vehicles in 2016, which represents a 32% increase in just four years. That is freight worth £119Billion, or 17% of the UK's total trade in goods. On 23 November last year, the port handled 10,558 freight vehicles in one day, or something like one vehicle every four seconds. If you lined them all up they would stretch up the M2, all the way round the M25 and up the M11 as far as Cambridge. So the border, and the port has to remain open and flexible if we are to avoid a catastrophic drop in our trade. And that necessity means, of course, some limitation on security. You simply cannot check all of the documents and/or search an HGV in four seconds. And bear in mind that a four second delay would halve the number of vehicles using the port. So Brexit brings some significant challenges for our Border Agency and military from sea access to our ports alone.

Next, military aid to the civilian power is fairly traditional in Britain. The Olympics, fireman's strike, national emergencies of one kind or another, can always rely on our army turning out and doing their bit in floods, fire, natural or manmade disaster. But whereas in days of yore we could have been confident of dealing with an emergency more or less wherever it occurred in the UK, or even if in several places simultaneously, I would be far less confident of being able to do so today. If – heaven forfend – there were to be a terrorist outrage in two, five, or seven places in Britain, would our military or police really be able to cope? I fear not.

Far more important than conventional defence against an attacker against these shores, and even more important than nuclear deterrence which is so vitally important in the world, but probably not in the context of the UK's onshore territories, is at least an attempt to defend ourselves against that modern form of aggressor – the terrorist. No-one predicted, nor, of course, prevented, the 9/11 outrage against the US, 7/7 bombings in London, nor Charlie Hebdo, the downing of the Russian jet in Sharm el Sheikh, the 37 Brits killed on the beach in Tunisia nor those in Paris, Manchester, London, Barcelona, Turkey. Terrorist outrages across the Middle East, Europe, Indonesia and much of the world are becoming commonplace – barely even registering the top slot on the evening news.

The world stood in stark horror at the appalling events in Paris's Charlie Hebdo and Bataclan, for example. The sheer barbarity of the murders of innocent people;

the terrorising of a nation and beyond; the despicable attempt to silence the press and thinkers – all of these are beyond words despicable. We are right to be heart-broken, outraged and concerned about the future in equal measure. But what should we now be thinking and doing in its aftermath? Let's start with a few things we should NOT be doing.

First, any attempt to make party political capital out of the tragedy – by Marine le Pen in France, and let's be frank, some elements of our own political spectrum – is a disgrace. Any increase in Islamophobia is exactly what these terrorist murderers want. They would love a crusade by the infidel against Islam if that can possibly be triggered off. We must not give them that satisfaction. These murders were carried out by a few mad fanatics, not by Islam. You could not blame IRA atrocities on the Roman Catholic Church. No more can you blame this on the Muslim faith. All but a very small minority of Muslims are decent, honourable, peace-loving people and must not be demonised.

Second, the pen-waving crowds at the post Charlie Hebdo outrage, led symbolically by Presidents Mahmud Abbas of Palestine and Benjamin Netanyahu of Israel arm in arm, were demonstrating against the blatant attempt to censor our free press. ISIL do not like the cartoons that Charlie Hebdo was carrying. They should have countered with words or with cartoons of their own, not with the bullet and the bomb. Equally, we must not allow their crimes to lead to interference in our freedoms. We may be uneasy about the intelligence services monitoring our electronic data, but I will go along with it if it makes significant difference to our security. We already have some of the best and toughest security measures anywhere in the world, but this kind of outrage shows that they need any help they can get to keep us safe.

And third, we must realise that this is but a symptom – an excrescence – of the much greater evil across the Middle East. ISIL, Al Qaeda, and other extremist Jihadists have a generational plan, which moderate and true Muslims must find a way to thwart. Only long-term peace and stability throughout the region – which is at present a million miles away – can hope to eliminate this wickedness.

It must be an Arab and Islamic solution to an Arab and Islamic problem. Yet we in the West must be ready to do whatever we can - in diplomatic, trade, financial, and military terms – to help them find that solution. The Middle East today is like the Balkans in 1912, or Western Europe in 1938 or so. Unless we can help to find a way through it, we will without doubt be facing a military catastrophe in the next ten years, which will make some of these outrages seem tame by comparison. Our statesmen and leaders must now tread very gently, and we must support them in it if we are to avoid that global catastrophe.

The Barcelona incident prompted me to write in my excellent local paper, the *Wiltshire Gazette and Herald*:

"The World reels from yet another Jihadi Daesh outrage – this time in Barcelona, but no different to Paris, Berlin, Brussels, London, Manchester or so many other places. Our hearts go out to the Spanish and to the bereaved and injured. We grieve, and we are resolute in never giving in to terrorism, and carrying on with our everyday lives as a kind of mark of defiance. All of those things are good and true and noble. But the trouble is that they just don't work. No matter how many candlelight vigils, streets strewn with flowers we see, these evil people see a soft West, and a West which can be defeated by their wicked and violent tactics.

"These people understand only one thing – strength. That has been proved throughout Iraq where Daesh are now virtually destroyed, and very nearly in Syria too. The Jihadi Caliphate was destroyed there by force of arms, by sheer power. Yet unless we also destroy the ideology, and cut off their source of funding, this multi-headed hydra will just go to ground under the sand, and will without doubt reappear in all its ugliness elsewhere in the Middle East or Africa, and most certainly in yet more high streets in our Western cities.

"We need to deal with their ideology at grass roots level. And we must be clear and firm. People who are returning from Iraq and Syria, for example, must be carefully quizzed by MI5. And if it turns out that they have been fighting for ISIS, they must either be thrown out of our country, or at very least have their passports removed and after due process of law they must be thrown into prison. Those people who the security forces know to be suspect must be investigated, irrespective of their bogus human rights claims; those who are in prison should be sent back to wherever they came from irrespective of the regime in their home country.

"And we must strengthen our delicate western liberal consciences over such things as surveillance. I don't mind being watched, and anyone hacking into my phone or computer would find nothing more interesting than a shopping list. We must be ready to lay the blame where it lies, and be outspoken and clear about it.

"Walking on politically correct egg-shells will not prevent another Barcelona, or Manchester. Locking these bad people up, or throwing them out of the country, may well help towards it, even if it bruises a few of our delicate Western sensibilities in doing so."

I received a deluge of email support for these views.

Appalling as that is, and demanding of whatever action may be needed to prevent it happening again, it may just be worth pondering for a moment how many more unspeakable outrages might have occurred had we not been doing what we can in action against Al Quaida in Afghanistan, against Daesh in Iraq and Syria, and in so many other less high profile ways around the world. (And no, our military actions in those places can't be blamed for the upsurge in terrorism, which of course had started well before any kind of military action on our part.)

Should we just accept the inevitability of further terrorist outrages? Should we really use the excuse of worries about increasing their ire and determination to act against us as an excuse for doing nothing about it? Surely not even the most ardent pacifist would advance that particular argument. We know that there are evil people in the Middle East and elsewhere both murdering people in the most brutal of ways, including many British people overseas, and without a doubt planning outrages of all sorts within the borders of the UK What would the reaction be if a dirty bomb of some kind in central London killed 1000 people, and the Government admitted that they had failed to act against the perpetrators while they could have done so at their home bases in Syria, Libya and elsewhere?

Op Shader – the largely RAF and partly army operation against Daesh in Iraq and Syria – is as crucial to the safety of our people onshore in the UK as was the Battle of Britain in1939. If we do not degrade and ultimately defeat Daesh, it is only a matter of time before we see more and more attacks by them or their sympathisers in mainland Britain. And the nature and severity of those attacks, encouraged by our failure to react to them, would become more and more severe. Not acting against Daesh would be to condemn a potentially large number of our countrymen to a horrible death or maiming.

All of that, of course, is without even touching on our revulsion at their murderous activities which we saw on our screens on an almost daily basis. Who could stand by and do nothing (or leave it to others to react on our behalves) to beheadings of aid workers and journalists, to the enslavement and mass rape of women, and their murder, to the sight of homosexual men being thrown off high rise buildings for their 'crime', to children being used as human shields, or even more revoltingly being brain-washed into carrying out the brutal killings themselves? Who could fail to be revolted by the ethnic cleansing, the racism, the sheer brutal intolerance of other religions we witnessed across Iraq and Syria. These are evils of a kind the world has not seen for a generation, and we could not have looked our children and grandchildren in the eye if we had not done something about it.

The Defence of the Realm against terror is just as real and just as important as it used to be against any potential aggressor lining up his bombers and landing craft in Calais in preparation for invasion. And defeating terrorism and seeking to prevent any such outrage on our shores is just as valid a military aim as would any such land defence.

Defence of our homeland requires a complex mix of military and intelligence assets. Conventional air power is obvious. So are target acquisition assets; special forces in one way or another, ISTAR in all its varied applications. But so are conventional skills and assets. The British Army, for example, have played a pivotal role in training the brave Peshmerga, Kurdish forces in Kurdistan to the north-east of Iraq. Conventional military training is something we are very good at, and the Peshmerga played a key role in reversing the advances which Daesh made in Iraq in 2014, and in the recapture of Mosul. We are training (and to a limited degree) equipping, the Iraqi forces as well, and may well do so in one role or another in the war against Daesh in Syria. And our newly-built naval base in Bahrain is not accidental.

So defence of the homeland is our first duty, and it needs both extensive conven-

NATO Headquarters in Brussels.

tional alongside all kinds of modern high tech military strengths to achieve it.

Close behind the Homeland must come mutual defence of our allies, especially NATO. Article 5 of the NATO Treaty stipulates that *"...an armed attack against one or more of them in Europe or North America shall be considered an attack against them all,"* and we of course are very likely to be the net beneficiaries of it. America is by far the largest and most powerful of all NATO members, contributing 3.61% of her GDP to defence, including but not limited to NATO. We Brits are one of only three other NATO countries who have achieved the 2% norm which they stipulate, other NATO nations falling far behind. France is on 1.78%, for example, Germany 1.19%, Italy 1.11%, Canada 0.99%

What all of that means, of course, is that to a greater or lesser degree all of the NATO members rely on the United States for their defence. However, America has in the last year or two indicated that they are 'pivoting' their attention to the Pacific and away from their Atlantic allies, calling as a result for more NATO colleagues to step up to the 2% defence spending plate. There is always a risk that at some stage in the future, and always depending on what is happening in the world, and especially in the Far East and Pacific, that America would start to reduce their contribution to NATO. *"Members {of NATO} must finally contribute their fair share and meet their obligations",* President Trump told the NATO heads of State, who were reported to be shuffling uneasily and staring at their feet (CNN). *"23 of the 28 member nations are still not paying what they should be paying... This is not fair to the people and taxpayers of the United States".* Yet any reduction in US defence spending, or even worse, any suggestion that she might withdraw from NATO, or even draw down a little leaving the European nations to shoulder more of the responsibility would have catastrophic consequences for the satisfactory defence of the U.K.

Now while I am by no means predicting a US withdrawal from NATO, which would have catastrophic consequences for the rest of the world, it is surely only right that we do what we can to prevent any diminution in their contribution occurring by doing our bit in defence of our own interests and nations. Excessive reliance on Uncle Sam (which of course has been the case at least since the First World War) might well be a long-term mistake, or at least we should do our bit to try to make him more comfortable with the contribution he is making to the better defence of our interests.

There are, on the other hand, those who would argue that our obligations to EU partner nations, even after Brexit (or perhaps especially after Brexit) is as important and as binding as those to NATO. I personally would not agree. There is no mutually binding EU military treaty equivalent to the NATO one. And I anyhow, I frankly would not want to rely on some EU countries in the event of some minor, or even major, attack on the UK. The Belgian Government's refusal even to SELL us ammunition at the time of the Falklands War gives one little confidence. Those of us who prefer to think of the EU as largely a trading mechanism, would argue that leaving aside a few mutually beneficial military tasks, such as the counter-piracy operation off Somalia, there should be no military nor diplomatic role for the EU whatsoever. It risks undermining NATO and potentially wastefully duplicating their efforts. The EU should be about trade, NATO about warfare and defence.

Our primary, and linked, duties of defence of the homeland and of our NATO allies demands substantial conventional, nuclear, cyber and unconventional assets and spending. The government's commitment to spending 2% of our wealth on defence is very well welcome, and (despite a few accounting quibbles) seems quite genuine. It is probably just about enough to fulfil the basic requirements of defending these shores, and of making our fair contribution to defending NATO.

But while welcoming that 2% commitment, currently around £45 Billion, it should not allow for any kind of complacency. Current defence spending is, after all, as low as we have ever known it. In 1947 it stood at 16% of GDP. It was 11.2% in 1950, 7% in 1963; 5.4% in 1970; and remained at 4% or over until the 1990s. By 1997 it was at 3%, sliding continuously under Labour and Tories alike to its current low point today of 2%. So there's no room for complacency there, and most defence and foreign affairs analysts believe that around 3% would better suit today's threats.

That 2% (or £45 billion, count it how you will), also has an important side benefit to our economy. Britain today remains – perhaps despite our best efforts – one of the world's greatest defence manufacturing nations. Companies like BAE Systems, Rolls Royce and others still lead the world. Their crucially important research and development capabilities are to a degree cross-subsidised by MOD defence equipment purchases. And, of course, through defence exports they also make a huge contribution to righting our Balance of Trade with the rest of the world.

While 2% is all very well, we should be clear that it will not necessarily deliver all that we would want it to. The world is a more dangerous place than we have known it for generations, yet we are spending less on our defence than for generations. An army of 82,000 men, barely uplifted as was promised by up to 30,000 reservists, a Navy of 19 surface ships is still pretty inadequate, even while welcoming the magnificent Queen Elizabeth class aircraft carriers which will indeed be our flagships for decades to come; and the RAF with 200 or so fighter aircraft and a total of only 33,000 personnel is barely able to carry out the very limited tasks being set for it in Syria and Iraq. Our equipment tends to be amongst the best, but our manpower has without doubt been 'hollowed out.' We could not carry out an operation like the Falklands nor Gulf 1 today, and simultaneous operations of the kind we fought in Iraq and Afghanistan only ten years ago would be wildly beyond our capabilities.

Now what all of that means is that even if we can be reasonably confident of defending our shores against aggressors of most kinds, even if we can be fairly proud of our contribution to NATO, we cannot hope to carry out wider military ambitions in the world. And it is important that government, and the people should recognise that that is the case.

We would be hard pressed, for example, to make much of a contribution to any large-scale humanitarian crisis, in Africa or elsewhere. We are seemingly powerless to deter Assad from murdering thousands of his own people with barrel bombs. We can do precious little about the tens of millions of people who are as a result homeless refugees, many of them starving or dying of the cold. 20,000 a year allowed into Britain is welcome, but a tiny pin-prick by comparison with the vast humanitarian and refugee crisis which is being played out before our eyes across the Middle East and large parts of North Africa. And the size of our military makes it impossible to imagine ever being able to do so.

We can most certainly not contemplate any military operation in support of our Western values and ideologies. We believe in democracy, and a free liberal economy. We believe in freedom of speech, protection for minorities, rights of women and of workers, an end to the death penalty and abhorrent sharia penalties such as stoning of prostitutes, dismembering of shoplifters and execution of dissidents and homosexuals. We would like to end those things which are so abhorrent to us, but we have no military capability to do so.

We can most certainly not be the world's policeman (and perhaps our people would not want us to be anyhow), nor really much of a force for good in the world. Trident and our nuclear deterrent together with our reasonable contribution to NATO still ensures our place at the military and diplomatic top tables – the UN

Security Council P5, and as part of the Special Relationship with the US. But at least one of our major political parties seems increasingly to be moving towards unilateralism, and some perfectly respectable defence thinkers occasionally argue that we should only be using our resources for those things that we are really good at and are demonstrably within our means – ISTAR and special forces, drones and the like.

And perhaps more important than any of that, we are perilously close to being unable to show sufficient military force to deter our potential enemies. Russia will without doubt constantly test our resilience and determination. So, in almost as sophisticated a way, do Daesh and other terrorists. If we are not strong, and are not SEEN to be strong, we will pay a heavy price for it. Up until now we have probably done our best, and just about achieved a reasonable level of deterrence. But it is a very thin line of defence, which a truly determined enemy could quite easily breach. There is most certainly no room for complacency.

Britain was quite demonstrably a great military nation in the past. Indeed, a large part of our 'greatness' is directly attributable to our military strength. The empire depended on our trading abilities, which of course wholly came about as a result of the Royal Navy. Our army – a million strong and more – both fought the great wars of history, but also patrolled the world. Irrespective of our modern dislike of empire, it was that military strength which truly made us 'Great' in a way which at the time at least was viewed with awe by the whole of the rest of the world. And it is plain to me that we cannot hope to regain that 'greatness' without at least some element of replication of that military might. America knows that, the Chinese know it in spades. We seem to think that we can be one of the world's great powers without actually making the financial and military commitment which being a great power requires. We are playing a big boy's game with a small boy's toys.

14. So Will We Ever Go To War Again?

"To be prepared for war is one of the most effective means of preserving peace."
(George Washington)

"I must study politics and war that my sons may have liberty to study mathematics and philosophy."
(John Adams)

"The supreme art of war is to subdue the enemy without fighting."
(Sun Tzu)

No-one likes war. No-one wants it. Yet leaving aside out and out pacifists, who perfectly honourably argue that all warfare and all armaments are wicked and should be abolished, most reasonable people would probably accept that occasional expeditionary warfare or military action will always be necessary as long as there are wicked people in the world.

At the very minimum, most would very probably go along with the motto of my own old regiment, the Honourable Artillery Company, *'Arma Pacis Fulcra.'* – Arms are the Balance of Peace. That is the essence of deterrence. There will always be bad people in the world, people ready to invade other countries, to carry out humanitarian atrocities. They are the very people with massive armouries of weapons, sometimes nuclear ones, often chemical or biological.

Yet they are also classic bullies – people who understand one thing and one thing only – massive counterbalancing force. Maggie Thatcher and Ronald Reagan won the Cold War because the Soviet Union knew that whatever they did would be met by overwhelming retaliation. Had the women peace-camp protesters around Greenham Common been successful and disarmed the UK, do you really think that Communism would have been all but destroyed?

Equally today, do you really think that Mr Putin respects a soft diplomatic approach? Of course he does not. He understands Article 5 of the NATO Treaty – which promises a collective military response to armed aggression against any member of the Alliance. That is why President Trump's undermining of Article 5, particularly with reference to the Baltic States is so very worrying.

Last year, I laid a wreath at the Moscow Tomb of the Unknown Warrior. Its discarded cape and helmet and rifle; the everlasting flame framed by the massive red walls of the Kremlin is a stunningly moving and beautiful memorial to the foolishness and pointlessness of war. It records the hundreds of thousands of deaths of young men in the war against Hitler, and neighbouring stones commemorate the great battles – Moscow, Leningrad, Kiev, Odessa, Stalingrad, Minsk and so many more. I was strangely moved by the thought of these thousands of young men from a far distant land who died in a war against our common enemy.

I was in Moscow for a couple of days with the Commons Defence Committee for discussions with the Russian Government, journalists, NGOs and foreign ambassadors about how we can lessen current tensions with NATO; about the annexation of Crimea and invasion of eastern Ukraine, about tensions in the Baltic States and around Kaliningrad. The fact of the matter is that tensions between Russia and the West are now running higher than at any time, and the risk of a (perhaps accidental) military exchange is very real. Even more chilling is the Russian view that 'tactical' nuclear weapons may reasonably be used to de-escalate a crisis. Our mission was to try to open channels for greater dialogue with the West with a view to de-escalation, or at least some degree of mutual understanding. But I have to admit that I detected little enthusiasm for doing so at least from the Russian side. And there are some pretty hawkish messages coming from NATO too. So we can expect further military skirmishes, like the two Russian planes who illegally and dangerously buzzed the USS *Donald Cook* in the Black Sea recently; we will see more Bear bombers testing our defences over UK airspace; we can expect Russian submarines exploring new waters, Russian paratroopers exercising at the North Pole as they did recently.

These are dangerous times indeed, and military escalation of the kind we will see in the next few years can do no-one any good. We must talk and talk; *'Jaw, jaw, jaw, not war, war, war.'* And if they won't talk, then a degree of ignoring them may well be an alternative route to de-escalation. Masterful strategic inaction, perhaps?

Those who would tell us that the only thing that President Putin understands is military strength, and who argue therefore for substantial re-armament, especially in the East and North of Europe, should take time out, as we did, to visit the Tomb of the Unknown Warrior, and contemplate the senseless loss of life which all warfare entails. Round the eternal flame, a motto (in Russian) reads "Your name is unknown; your deed is immortal." Let their immortality be a remembrance of the awfulness of war, and a renewed determination to avoid it.

Having said all of which, do you really think that those vicious murdering swine, Daesh, are going to stop throwing gay men off sky-scrapers, raping Christian women and indiscriminately murdering anyone they believe to be an apostate through gentle persuasion? Undoubtedly they will not. They will understand – and feel the effects of – nothing but overwhelming force.

Arms are the Balance of Peace.

But there have emerged in recent years four obstacles which might well prevent any expeditionary warfare, any intervention overseas, no matter how justifiable and right such action would in reality be. They are also obstacles which fundamentally

Royal Wootton Bassett Repatriation.

call into question this deterrence effect of our arms and armies.

First, the general public, on both sides of the Atlantic and around the world, are much less clear than they used to be about the purpose of warfare. While the British public have a very high regard for our military personnel and all they do, they have a historically poor understanding or even regard for what they have to do. The people of Royal Wootton Bassett in my constituency turned out on 167 occasions in all weathers to honour a total of 345 coffins as they were carried down their High Street. Their respect for our armed forces and their sacrifices is second to none. But it would be wholly wrong to imagine that their Repatriation Ceremonies week by week signified any kind of support for, or even real understanding of, what we had been doing in Afghanistan and Iraq. People talk of 'our brave boys and girls' but they actually mean that they would prefer them to be back in barracks at home rather than risking their lives engaged in military activity abroad. In other words, there is a bigger, and most worrying, disconnect than ever before between respect for our armed forces – which is at an all-time high; and respect and support for what governments are asking them to do – which is at an all-time low.

Afghan border: Do not cross.

Camp Bastion, War Memorial, Afghanistan, 2007.

The end of warfare in Afghanistan and Iraq and the sour taste left in our mouths in their aftermath, has removed any possible popular appetite for expeditionary warfare. No matter what happens in the world now, would we really persuade a sceptical public to intervene in it? Probably not. Let us hope that we find a peaceful diplomatic solution to Syria, Ukraine, Central African Republic, Pakistan, and so many other global flashpoints. I hope that we do, but have very little confidence that we will. But I would not want to be the Prime Minister seeking to explain to a sceptical public why we should engage in any form of military intervention in any of those places or many like them. David Cameron's shambolic Syria vote on 29 August, 2013 may well be a stark warning of similar votes to come in the future. No matter how worthwhile or even necessary the proposed military action in Syria may or may not have been (and that is a matter for a separate discussion), there was no way in the world that he would have achieved a majority for it in the House of Commons. A year before a General Election, an MP defending a majority of – let us say – a hundred votes, pays a great deal of attention to the thousand emails he or she might have received opposing some piece of expeditionary warfare.

There is a powerful feeling around that we are at last bringing our military home – both from Afghanistan and from Germany – and that we want them hunkered down in their barracks, their main function being to defend our homelands. Something of the same can be said of popular opposition to the UK's record high spending on overseas aid. The people want to retreat behind our castle with the drawbridge firmly pulled up behind us, and turn our backs on world events.

The purpose and aims of wars used to be straightforward. One nation upset another; one king wanted a bit of territory; diplomats and emissaries issued demands and ultimatums; if they failed, war was declared, then waged; one side or the other won; a peace treaty was negotiated; land or money changed hands, and the course of history rolled on.

William, Duke of Normandy, invaded England; the Saxons tried their best to defend themselves but lost (at least partly because the Normans understood the use of stirrups to enable the cut and thrust from horseback; the Saxons, having none, were forced to fight dismounted!); and the Normans took over England.

Hitler invaded Poland; the PM's deadline passed and war was declared; it continued until the unconditional surrender of Germany six years later. The Argentinians invaded the Falklands; British forces threw them out again. Saddam Hussein invaded Kuwait; an outraged international community threw him out.

Things still seemed pretty simple when terrorists hijacked some airliners on 11 September 2001 and slammed into New York's World Trade Centre and the Pentagon in Washington DC, with a terrible loss of life and an even more dramatic effect on America's nationhood and self-respect. Their military reaction was straightforward and predictable.

Less than a month later, on 7 October 2001, American and British troops invaded Afghanistan. The justification was pretty obvious and universally agreed. Osama bin Laden, the leader of Al Qaeda, who was self-confessedly responsible for the 9/11 outrage, was based in a cavernous hide-out in the Bora Bora Mountains in Southern Afghanistan. Since the Soviet withdrawal, Afghanistan had become more and more lawless and ever more a base for international terrorism. There were terrorist training camps there.

A military reaction against Afghanistan was fair and reasonable in anyone's eyes. But it was an operation which could and should have been carried out with massive force in three to six months. It would by that means both have helped to assuage Middle America's outrage, and, it was to be hoped, would also have had a dramatic effect on world terrorism through the destruction of one of its heartlands, and a powerful deterrence to others who might have similar attacks in mind. *"Pour encourager les autres"* as Voltaire would have said.

Yet fifteen years later and after thousands of British, American and Afghan deaths, we are really no closer to understanding what it was that we were trying to do there than we were at the very beginning.

I remember a classic army PowerPoint presentation on our operations in Afghanistan on a visit to the troops in Helmand Province in 2007/8. Having explained what they were doing (and doing so well), the Brigadier concluded with a series of slides designed to justify the army's long-term presence in Afghanistan. A grinning farmer held up a sheaf of wheat to demonstrate our successful war against drugs (the largest opium crop of all time was nonetheless harvested in Afghanistan in 2013). The vast power generator carried at enormous price to the Kijacki Dam was the next slide – and the Brigadier cannot have known that seven or eight years later it would lie rusting where he left it. The final slide was of two grinning school-girls, jotters firmly clamped under their arms on their way to school.

"And that, ladies and gentlemen," said the Brigadier," is what it's all about. Security, infrastructure improvements, poppy destruction and girls' education."

I hope I was not being difficult or discourteous when I asked:

"Thank you, Brigadier. Very instructive. And can you just remind me which aspect of international law allows us to deploy tens of thousands of troops in a foreign country in pursuit of better education for girls?"

"Er...well. Um....Good point. Isn't that a matter for you politicians?" the Brigadier mumbled.

It was quite plain then – and now – that we really had very little strategic justi-fication for our long-term deployment in Afghanistan.

We had, if anything, even less justification for our invasion of Iraq eighteen months after 9/11.

On 20 March 2003, thousands of US and British troops crossed the bund from Kuwait into Iraq. They really had very little idea why they were doing so. Saddam, so far as we know, played no part whatsoever in 9/11. His regime was secular rather than Islamic. He had no loyalties to Osama bin Laden nor Al Qaeda. Bin Laden and Saddam were in many ways at opposite extremes.

So why did we invade Iraq in the aftermath of 9/11? Really no-one knows. Tony Blair and his 'Dodgy Dossier' focussed on Weapons of Mass Destruction about which he claimed intelligence alleging vast quantities being ready for deployment within forty-five minutes. That he must have known that to be untrue did not deter him from using those arguments in statements to the House of Commons and elsewhere in a desperate effort to justify what he was doing.

On other occasions, Foreign Secretary Jack Straw sought to argue that it was for human rights purposes. He memorably described how prostitutes were allegedly stoned in the Baghdad streets as if somehow or another that justified what would otherwise have been a wholly illegal war. Why, as a QC, international lawyer and Foreign Secretary, he thought that human rights violations of the kind he was describing (even if they actually occurred) justified an invasion of a sovereign terri-tory is hard to imagine.

Why the Government separately sought to justify the war with Iraq as some kind of an integral part of the otherwise reasonable 'War on Terror' is equally hard to fathom. Iraq was not part of the international terrorist networks – unlike her deadly enemy Iran. There was probably less terrorism emanating from Iraq than from almost any other Middle Eastern country, and a principal effect of the war against Saddam Hussein has been to create a brand-new breeding-ground for terrorists in Iraq. Yet the invasion and the thousands of lives subsequently lost formed the main part of the 'War on Terror.' Why?

The Chilcot Report into the causes, run-up and conduct of the Operation Telic in Iraq was a long-time-coming, but it was well worth waiting for. Those who had confidently predicted a 'whitewash' were thoroughly disappointed, as were those seeking a witch-hunt scapegoating of certain individuals. It is a well-balanced, carefully argued and evidenced analysis of what went wrong in 2003 – the decision-making; the conduct of the war; and our complete failure to plan for the post-conflict reconstruction of Iraq, for which we will pay a full and heavy price for many years to come.

Tony Blair's informal sofa-style Government; his slavish subservience to President Bush; his obsession with 'spin' and 'presentation' at the expense of substance and veracity took us into what was clearly, in my view, an illegal war. It is true that Chilcot did not quite say so, not least because it was beyond his remit. But I am glad that I resigned as Shadow Defence Minister over what was, in my view, a deeply flawed decision. I will, however, always kick myself that I was persuaded by the whips to abstain in the vote on the war rather than vote against the government.

Incidentally, one outcome seems to me plain: that a vote in the House of Commons on war by no means guarantees that it is legal or justifiable. Indeed, as I argued in my book *Who Takes Britain to War?* (History Press, 2015) by whipping MPs into supporting a war you are by that very means removing their right and ability to challenge the government on it. Rather than empowerment, a Parliamentary vote could become emasculation.

I remember visiting the front line in Iraq in 2003 shortly after the invasion, and being struck by the inadequacies of some elements of our troops' equipment, at least partly as a result of the very short lead in time which Mr Blair's shenanigans gave them. Several of the bodies so sadly repatriated through Royal Wootton Bassett High Street were needless deaths caused by the inadequacy of certain equipment. That lesson must be firmly learned by the MOD.

Destroying Al Qaida may be more or less justifiable. Protecting the West from terrorist attack seems reasonable, but regime change? Drugs? Girls' education? Hydroelectric schemes and preventing prostitutes being stoned in the streets? By no stretch of anyone's imagination could these things justify high intensity kinetic warfare of the kind we experienced in Iraq and Afghanistan for fifrteen years or so.

Yet UK and US troops having finally left Afghanistan at the end of 2014, do we really know whether or not the massive price paid in 'blood and treasure' was justified? Did we win? Did we achieve something which future generations will recognise as having been demonstrably worth it? I doubt it.

We have at our disposal today the deadliest weaponry in the history of mankind; we have the greatest ability of all time to deploy it anywhere we care at extraordinarily short notice. Weapons and the military today have greater capacity than ever – for good or ill – around the Globe. Yet we have really very little idea what to do with it or why. We are little boys blundering around the nursery playing with big boys' toys.

So surely it is time that we sat down with a cold towel around our collective heads and worked out what warfare is and what it can legitimately be used for. If we truly understood our military capacity in the West, and if we could discuss and codify what we believed was a legitimate use for it, we would be making credible steps towards working out a method of deciding on when and how to use these terrible capabilities.

Now some of this work is – and always has been – done by the world's militaries. They constantly struggle with the thinking and justification which lies behind what they do. Defence doctrine fills shelves in the library. They produce all sorts of Rules of Engagement under the Geneva Convention which curtail and control the way in which we use military capabilities. NATO, the UN, national governments have teams of civil servants struggling with the ideas; academics have produced acres of books and articles about it all. Yet despite that we are as unclear today about why and how we go to war as we ever were. The justification and conduct of Iraq and Afghanistan were questionable in the extreme; Kosovo was conducted without UN sanction; Vietnam was a catastrophic failure.

The civilised West really has very little idea of how and why we go to war, and that is despite several thousand years of efforts by philosophers to codify, to write down, what warfare is, what it should be, and how it can be justified. Discussion about the 'Just War' has preoccupied philosophers from the ancient Greeks, through St Thomas Aquinas, Clausewitz and up to modern times. And much modern law of conflict, from the Geneva Conventions and downwards, is based on that philosophical work.

In a similar way, perhaps we should now seek to codify what we as a nation and a generation believe to be a 'Just War.' We should seek to produce a broadly agreed codification of when and why and how we believe it reasonable to deploy armed force around the world. If we could do that, we would be taking a major step towards working out the mechanism by which we agree to deploy that force.

Any such codification of the Just War would always have to be allowed to evolve over the generations and centuries. What was 'just' to the ancients, to mediaeval man, or even in the eighteenth or nineteenth centuries will almost certainly not be seen as 'just' today. Yet in any one era, surely it should be possible to produce a clearly expressed codification of what we believe the 'Just War' should be?

An aggressive alien assaulting our shores quite plainly justifies armed self-defence. Limited overseas intervention to prevent said aggressor ever reaching our shores presumably would be acceptable to most. The defence of our interests overseas – keeping shipping lanes open, defending natural resources on which we survive – is probably reasonable. Looking after British expatriates is certainly defensible. Upholding international treaties and agreements, carrying out the will of the UN Security Council, defending our fellow NATO states. All of these things would be widely – though inevitably not universally – accepted as being 'just'.

But what about intervening against a foreign dictator who is murdering or torturing his own people? We thought that fine against Hitler (although of course the Holocaust was never the reason for the war since in 1939 we knew nothing about it[1]); but Assad gassing a few hundreds of his people? We were not sure. What if we knew that a mad dictator was gassing hundreds of thousands of his people – or millions? Would our decision be different then? Is it a question of quantity? Or of principle? Most people appeared to feel the interventions in Kosovo and Sierra Leone were justified by the innocent lives they saved, though others disapproved. Many people criticised the West for not intervening in Rwanda to prevent the massacre of many more innocent people, though had we done so there would certainly have been other voices raised against the use of military force.

None of these questions are easy. Yet all are capable of coherent intellectual discussion. Surely it should be possible for an intelligent society through a process of national debate to agree what would be fair and reasonable in terms of warfare and what would not? Surely we could produce a codified definition of the 'Just War' at any one stage in our national development, albeit possibly necessary to amend that codification from time to time.

In other words, what I am suggesting is that we should now seek to produce a clearly expressed, nationally agreed document which lays out what we, the British people, believe is a reasonable use for our weaponry and armed forces. Doing so would prevent their improper use (Iraq, possibly Afghanistan). It would prevent their capricious or illegal use, and permit their legitimate use (Falklands, Kuwait). Finally it would clarify for the troops themselves what they were doing and why.

The British public were sold a pup in Tony Blair's Weapons of Mass Destruction in 2003. They see an Afghanistan which is little better today than before fifteen years or so of vicious fighting. There can be no denying that the appetite for military action has been blunted in the liberal West by the Afghanistan and Iraq experience. 'It didn't work there, so why should it work elsewhere?' is the simplistic question. It would indeed be a bold Prime Minister today,

---

[1] The murdering of his own people was never advanced as a justification for going to war with Hitler, the casus belli being the invasion of Poland with whom we had signed a treaty of mutual assistance. The casus belli for the Iraq War was WMD, but again Saddam's murder of the Marsh Arabs no doubt helped to make it more palatable.

especially one with a slender majority, who would propose to the nation any bar the most obvious, the most urgent and undeniable of military action. He or she would simply not get popular support for it; and without popular support, no Prime Minister could contemplate taking the country to war, nor putting our service people in the line of danger.

Today's electorate need to know that the proposed action is necessary, proportionate, will succeed, will be of overall benefit to the peace of the world, and that there will be some kind of plan for rebuilding after the kinetic warfare is over. Unless they are sure of those pre-conditions they will not support any government which in their view foolishly or needlessly risks our young men's lives in warfare.

And it is hard to imagine any possible threat or conflict today when those preconditions will be fulfilled. If Mr Putin were to invade Estonia, it is possible (despite Trump) to imagine reasonable support. But what if he were to position a company of troops in Norwegian-controlled Svalbard? Would the British people really support defensive action of an all-but uninhabited archipelago north of the Arctic Circle? Or would a Russian platoon occupying Swedish Gottland trigger popular support for expeditionary warfare? Very probably not, at least partly because Sweden is not a member of NATO. But if we did not do something about Svalbard or Gottland, would we not be risking our own security? If China were to position troops near Taiwan, which they have for forty years argued to be an integral part of mainland China, would we really enthusiastically support American armed aggression against China? Or if Boko Haram were to capture and murder hundreds of civilians in Northern Nigeria, would our constituents really thank us for trying to prevent further outrages in a UN peace-keeping mission?

Twenty-four hour rolling news and perhaps social media and the Internet has made us all greatly more aware of the world than were our immediate ancestors. We used to trust what our betters told us, accept that we were 'fighting for King and Country' and march off to war, very often having very little understanding of what we were fighting about. Since the effective formation of the United Kingdom in 1707, there have been 123 wars conducted by the British, 37 of them since 1900. I wonder how many of them would garner popular support today?

So the deterrence effect is first diminished by our lack of clarity as to Britain's position in the world; lack of popular support as a result for expeditionary warfare to cure the world's ills; and war-weariness post Iraq and Afghanistan.

The second obstacle to warfare after the demonstrable lack of public understanding of military force, and a total lack of popular enthusiasm for deploying it, comes from what might at first glance be thought to be a pretty unimportant constitutional change. Until 2003, The Prime Minister and Cabinet used the ancient 'Royal Prerogative' to take the country to war. Parliament and the people were kept fully up to date, and no military action would ever be politically possible without the support of Parliament and the people. But it was the Executive who decided and who were then held to account by Parliament. Since 2003, when for the first time ever the PM sought – and achieved – a vote in the House of Commons in favour of expeditionary warfare (against Saddam) there has been a developing (but not yet – quite – universally accepted) convention that, leaving aside any emergency, or any immediate threat to our shores, there should never be a premeditated deployment of troops without the support of the Houses of Parliament.

Since 2003, we voted down the PM's proposal to bomb of Assad in Syria, and supported his proposal to bomb ISIS in Iraq and then in Syria. There was no vote prior to the deployment against Libya, nor for any one of the 25 or so areas in which British troops are currently deployed overseas.

It is perhaps ironic that those MPs (like me) who are most distressed by the appalling scenes in Aleppo are those who, in a vote in the House of Commons in September 2013, prevented David Cameron from launching air strikes against Assad in retaliation for his use of chemical weapons against his own people. Knowing what we now know, would we do the same again? I very much doubt it. Likewise, those MPs who now most vocifer-

James Gray speaking in the chamber of the House of Commons.

ously agonise about Tony Blair's invasion of Iraq in 2003 are also those who voted in favour of it. He would most certainly not get a majority in favour today, no matter how hard he tried to whip it. With hindsight, the Libya campaign was a catastrophe. Yet would backbenchers have voted to support it? Surely not. And would they have been correct either way round? Who will ever know? And those who voted for airstrikes against ISIS in Iraq and then Syria worry to this day as to whether or not that was the right thing to have done. History will tell.

But one thing is for sure. A vote in the House of Commons on military action – either in favour or against it – is no guarantee of its correctness (or lack of it). Equally, the most justifiable and successful military actions and wars in history were conducted without any such Parliamentary vote. There was no vote on Gulf 1 when we repelled Saddam from Kuwait, nor on the Falklands, nor on any part of the Balkans, nor on the Second World War. Indeed in the long history of warfare, there have been only four substantive votes in the House, all of them to a greater or lesser degree questionable, while countless successful and easily justifiable military campaigns were conducted with the House of Commons being their scrutineer and holding the Prime Minister and government to account over them rather than being their instigator by voting for them.

Securing a vote prior to deployment has in a very real way emasculated Parliament. If we MPs have voted for it, can we really then criticise its motives or conduct? That we need a vote in the House of Commons prior to any such expeditionary warfare – a vote which might or might not be achieved – must also fundamentally undermine the deterrence effect of possible expeditionary warfare.

It is hard to imagine the Royal Prerogative genie being put back in its bottle. The Parliamentary Convention of a vote prior to deployment is now ten years old, and seems widely accepted by all bar those who have truly thought it through. However if it cannot be reversed, or if it cannot be replicated by some kind of War Powers Act akin to the American version (which brings all kinds of associated legal risks), then surely it is vanishingly unlikely that there will ever be any form of premeditated expeditionary warfare ever again. MPs will simply not vote for it - especially those with slim majorities, or perhaps facing reselection by their local party. No government will ever again achieve a majority for any war bar the blindingly obvious. Expeditionary warfare and the deterrence effect of its threat must by definition therefore be severely curtailed.

[Note: These arguments are further explained in my sister book, *Who Takes Britain to War?* (History Press 2016, reprinted 2018)]

For expeditionary warfare to be undertaken, it is, third, essential that our military should be able to carry out their orders relatively untrammelled by concerns as to whether or not what they are doing is legal. It always used to be that, leaving aside the Geneva Conventions for the proper conduct of war, which are clear and well-known, the military could carry out their orders, certain in the legal justification of what they were doing. But recent experience of the creep of 'lawfare' is making the proper conduct of expeditionary warfare ever more difficult. It is becoming harder and harder to conduct any form of conventional warfare because of international legal constraints.

As Lord Justice Moses says in his introduction to a recent Policy Exchange paper by Thomas Tugendhat MP and Laura Croft (*The Fog of Law, an introduction to the legal erosion of British Fighting Power*), *"None have succeeded in defeating the armed forces of the United Kingdom. Napoleon, Falkenhayn and Hitler could not. But where these enemies failed, our own legal institutions threaten to succeed."* By a majority of four to three, the UK's Supreme Court ruled in June 2013 that Article 2 of the European Convention on Human Rights should apply to soldiers in the field of battle. As Tughendhat and Croft argue *"The customs and practices of Britain's armed forces are now under threat from an unexpected quarter: the law. Recent legal developments have undermined the armed forces ability to operate effectively on the battlefield."* They go on to describe *"legal siege, legal entitlement, judicial creep and even Lawfare"* and to argue that fear of prosecution in the International Courts risks significantly undermining our national ability to commit troops to war.

We have chosen (until perhaps recently) not to derogate from the European Convention on Human Rights with regard to overseas expeditions, making our soldiers subject to the vagaries of the ECHR. The International Criminal Court in the Hague hovers over anything which even slightly smells of a 'war crime.' Perhaps in an effort to protect ourselves from them, we British established the Iraq Historic Allegations Tribunal, which turned out to be a classic witch-hunt. Some 4000 soldiers who carried out their duties in Iraq with no hint of criminal activity, nonetheless many years later found themselves under investigation on the say-so of a company of lawyers, Leigh Day and their boss, Phil Shiner, who saw these allegations as some kind of a cash-cow. After seven years, the number, it is said will be reduced to 60, and probably only a handful of them will be found to have any case to answer. The only successful prosecution so far of this egregious organisation is one of their own employees. It has cost £70 million, ruined the lives of 4000 troops and their families, and it must cast a shadow over any kind of expeditionary warfare we may contemplate in the future. Who would want to join the army; who would want to point their rifle and fire at an advancing enemy; who would want to carry out their officers' orders if they knew that ten or twenty or thirty years afterwards they might find themselves in the criminal courts through no fault of their own? We are now proposing that we do something similar with regard to Afghanistan, and the Police Service of Northern Ireland, who have recently arrested and charged two paras for carrying out their duties during The Troubles, are proposing to re-open a host of other long-forgotten cases. Not only does that ignore the countless known and proven terrorists who are walking free under the Good Friday agreement; it also fundamentally undermines the willingness – and the ability – of our armed forces to carry out their very often very difficult expeditionary warfare duties.

And fourth, even if the first three hurdles to proper expeditionary warfare as a deterrence were by some miracle to be overcome, as we have seen in the previous chapter, it is increasingly obvious that we in the West simply do not have the resources for any bar the most limited of deployments. A regular army of 82,000 is the smallest since Waterloo; and total armed forces of 186,000 or so is pitifully small. The equivalent number was 350,000 throughout the Cold War, half a million long after the end of National Service, and of course up to 5 million during the Second World War.

Much play is made of our commitment to spending 2% of GDP on defence. Even leaving aside the suspicion of creative accounting to achieve that figure, it is the lowest spend on defence ever. 2% is an absolute basic minimum, below which we would not be able to defend these shores. Add to that the failure of all bar a few of our NATO allies even to achieving 2%, and Mr Trump's reluctance to go on 'subsidising' Europe's defence, and you face a significant shortfall in our ability to do anything very worthwhile on the world's stage. We simply do not have the military resources to do what we want to do, or even, perhaps, to carry out the most basic defence of our interests.

So for those four reasons – a lack of understanding of our role in the world; the awkward mechanics of securing a Parliamentary vote prior to any deployment; the creeping cancer of Lawfare debilitating our efforts at warfare; and the crippling of our capabilities by continual reduction in our defence spending – add all of those together and you have a most worrying inability to conduct proper expeditionary warfare of any kind. No matter what happens in the world we simply will not be willing, or able, to go to war to prevent it. The damage to deterrence is chilling. Our ability to do what is best for the world is being fatally undermined. Unless we do something urgent and dramatic and decisive about it, we will soon as a result no longer be able to consider ourselves a force for good in the world.

Post-Brexit we have a once-in-a-generation opportunity to rediscover ourselves as a truly great World Nation. That can only happen if we urgently address all four impediments to expeditionary warfare. What's more, all of that is happening at the same time as most of the rest of the world are increasing their defence spending, and more and more of the world is looking ever more dangerous.

There's an eerie echo here of the early 1930s when we disarmed, with Churchill as a lone voice warning against it. Are we not once again risking leaving ourselves unprotected against world developments and unable to play our historic part in influencing them for the good of humanity? Are we really unwittingly heading for Glorious Isolation? If so, that must at very least be a product of a clear and conscious decision by the people, rather than an almost unseen and coincidental result of concurrent pressures.

15.Britain: A Parliamentary Democracy

"The oppressed are allowed once every few years to decide which particular representatives of the oppressing class are to represent and repress them in parliament." (Vladimir Lenin)

We can be a great trading nation again. We can have truly global influence through our reinvigorated Foreign and Commonwealth Office, and our strategic and humanitarian overseas aid. We can achieve this if we once again strengthen our armed forces and remove some of the four obstacles to successful interventionist warfare. But we also have so much else to offer the world. Let's have a look at each of our strengths in turn.

There is something romantic, dashing, mysterious, and above all distant, about the very name "Outer Mongolia." Ghenghis Khan, the Silk Road, fierce horsemen, nomads in gers. (You must never call them 'yurts' in Mongolia – they hate that and all other Russian words. Ger is the Mongolian for their felt-clad circular, and remarkably warm and comfortable mobile homes.) It's a country twice the size of France, yet with a population of only two million, one third of whom are nomadic herdsmen. She has been invaded and dominated at various times in her history by her two gigantic and overbearing neighbours – China (who still control 'Inner Mongolia') and Russia (as part of the USSR for seventy years from 1924 to 1992). Yet from the fall of the Soviet Union in 1990, Mongolia has been a proudly independent republic, whose Great State Hural (parliament) bears more than a passing resemblance to Westminster. So here is a proud little republic, surrounded by two communist hegemonies, maintaining her fierce parliamentary democracy against all of the odds. It is quite right that the Inter Parliamentary Union, and the UK Parliament go to great lengths to maintain our links with them, (Britain was the first overseas country to open full diplomatic relations with Mongolia) and to help and nurture their democratic institutions.

It was in 1865 that Liberal Reformer John Bright first coined the phrase that *"England is the Mother of Parliaments"* which has so often, and so justifiably, been taken as meaning that our parliamentary system in the UK is indeed the Mother of Parliamentary systems throughout the world. Our Westminster Parliament was founded effectively by Simon de Montfort in 1265, although very much based on earlier meetings after King John's Magna Carta in 1215, and arguably descending from Anglo Saxon Moots and Witans as early as the eighth century. So our Parliament is based on the best part of 1000 years of evolution, which means that every part of it has been tried and tested, often changed, only once by revolution.

(It is beaten for longevity only by the Icelandic Thingvellir, which is said to have been the parliament from about 1000 to 1800 or so; and by the ancient borough of Malmesbury in my own constituency of North Wiltshire whose 'Old Corporation' was founded by King Athelstan in 934, thereby making them the oldest unit of local government in the world, and whose descendants by birth still meet three times a year in their ancient 'Court House' in Malmesbury.)

That longevity means that, warts and all, the British parliamentary system works, and works brilliantly well. It is unquestionable that if you were to sit down with a pencil and paper you would not necessarily design a new parliament like it, with all of its foibles and peculiarities. The House of Lords, in particular, with its 92 hereditary peers (who hold elections when one of their number die, making them the only elected peers), the bishops, the appointees; men in tricorn hats; The State Opening of Parliament and all of its pageant and flummery; Black Rod having the door banged ceremonially in his face, government and opposition facing each other in intentionally antagonistic style, people referring to each other in the third person, always using their constituencies rather than their name – these and a thousand other conventions and practices are the product of that evolutionary process. And my goodness me, it works. It really is the finest parliamentary system in the world, producing first class legislation, and holding the government of the day to account, whatever their political colour may be. It's a system which is virtually incapable of corruption of any sort; it is understandable, sensible and transparent. And it is a system which is the envy of most of the world.

The Westminster system in whole or in part has been used by: Antigua and Barbuda, Australia, The Bahamas, Bermuda, Bangladesh, Barbados, Belize, Canada, Dominica, Grenada, India, Ireland, Israel, Japan, Jamaica, Kuwait, Malaysia, Malta, Mauritius, Nauru, Nepal, New Zealand, Pakistan, Papua New Guinea, Saint Kitts and Nevis, Saint Lucia, Singapore, Saint Vincent and the Grenadines, Solomon Islands, Trinidad and Tobago, Tuvalu, and Vanuatu, and that is without counting countries like little Mongolia whose system is similar in many regards.

So misquotation it may be, but ours really is the Mother of Parliaments.

Yet over the last forty years or so, Parliament has become weak, emasculated and muddled. Brexit may be just the Viagra it needs. Our powers to scrutinise and hold to account the government have been eroded – by the EU, devolution to Scotland, Wales and local government, and twenty-four hour rolling news providing an Opposition singularly lacking elsewhere. That has suited the covert agenda of an increasingly powerful and centralised Executive who have found ways to tempt Parliament's backbenchers down harmless diversionary routes like pointless debates and non-parliamentary 'casework.'

We must never forget that Parliament's job is not to run the country but to scrutinise and hold to account those of its members who, by right of their Parliamentary majority, seek to do so by forming a government. It's about scrutinising Bills, and like them or loathe them, at least making them into good, work-able law. It's about keeping a watch on ministers through debates and question times, Select Committees and so much more. It's about holding them to account, holding their feet to the fire, and ensuring that all of those things which they do by ministerial dictat, unconnected with legislation, they do in the best interests of the nation as a whole. It's about shouting the corner for the unique local needs of the individual MP's own constituency; and it's about speaking up for minorities and for the weak, and for those unable to speak for themselves.

Parliament should be a powerful institution making ministers and civil servants quake in their boots, asking awkward questions, making themselves diffi-cult; ensuring that whatever the governing party promised in their election mani-festo is exactly – no less than and no more than – what they deliver in their five years in office.

Yet Tony Blair was the first PM to realise that the weaker Parliament is, the more unfettered will be ministers' freedom to act, and he took steps to further that erosion. It was under him that we first saw the near universal use of Parliamentary 'guillotines' – the time-limiting of debate. By that means, he abolished one of the few real weapons at the disposal of the opposition – time. We Conservatives voted against Timetable Motions for thirteen years arguing that they were a scourge of Parliamentary democracy. But in government, of course, we love them and have preserved and extended them. Time limits on speeches, which are a corollary of timetabling, means that we err on the side of quantity rather than quality. No matter how learned or distinguished, how expert or how impassioned a speaker may be, he or she gets the same three minutes allotted to the newest backbencher. Debates are pretty shabby little rags by comparison with the great old days of Thatcher, Churchill, Disraeli, and the quality of the legislation we send up to the Lords is as a result so poor that it demands dozens of amendments, many of them from the government itself, during the much more thorough Lords' scrutiny of our Bills.

Mr Blair's emasculation of Parliament went further. He used to send his back-benchers home for 'constituency weeks' and brought in bogus 'family friendly hours' to keep Parliament out of his hair. He brought in innocent amusements to keep the backbenchers happy. Debates in Westminster Hall – the second debating chamber – are worthy enough, but being incapable of a vote are in no way 'binding.' Even less so are the recent invention of debates on public petitions which give people the entirely false impression that if they raise more than 100,000 signatures, they will get a vote in Parliament. The 4 million who petitioned for a second EU Referendum must have been more than a little disappointed at three hours of discussion concluded by a wind-up from a junior minister. Regular Opposition Day Debates in the main chamber are either ignored or routinely voted down by government backbenchers who have not been present for much of the debate; and the fairly recent invention of 'Backbench Business Committee Debates' allows a good airing of some topic dear to an MP's heart, but has little effect on policy or governmental behaviour. They used to be more potent – the EU Referendum, for example, originated in one – but the government soon realised that the best way of dealing with awkward backbench debates was to ignore them. Today they are a dozy backwater on an ill-attended Thursday afternoon.

Debates and question times are largely formal and formulaic, the Prime Minister and ministers pay them little attention, numbers attending from the backbenches are low, debates end early through lack of speakers. Thursdays and Fridays have become largely non-days, populated by those who long for their youth in the Oxford and Cambridge Union, and who like debating for debating's sake.

Most MPs head for their constituencies on Wednesday nights, where an obliging government lavishes expenses on them to set up offices in the high street, and to employ large numbers of 'casework-ers' to man them. The more marginal the seat is, the keener we are to undertake massive 'casework' with an eye more to our parliamentary longevity and majority than anything to do with helping constituents with central government matters. We rush around receptions, meetings, brief-ings; we campaign; we make speeches no-one listens to.

Otis Ferry interrupts proceedings in the House of Commons.

Now they are keen to get rid of the visible signs and symbols of Parliament - the funny clothes, ancient traditions, wigs for the clerks at The Table; the long tradition of impartiality by the Speaker; the careful language, the powerfully influ-encing speeches, even the need for MPs to wear ties. Soon they will close the build-ing under guise of 'modernising it', making it more public-friendly and the rest of it. "Wigs? Away with them. Court Dress? Pish and Tush. Vellum to record our Acts? Consign it to the litter bin. Mr Speaker's robes and full-bottomed wig? Away with the folderol which would only suppress my personality in favour of the office. Clapping? Hear, Hear. MPs in jeans and t-shirts: bring it on. We are inclusive, open to all, unforbidding, above all un-stuffy." "And while we're at it let's get rid of men in tights as doorkeepers and send their Crown Jewel badges back to the Tower of London; lets melt down the mace and give the money to the poor. 'Hat's off strangers? Don't trouble yourselves; third person useage, right honourables, far less gallants or learneds; away with it all (except of course for due deference for our Speaker as he walks by or its off to the Tower with you.)"

Commons clerks in wigs.

The first known Speaker of the House of Commons was Wiltshire boy Sir Thomas Hungerford, who was MP for the area from 1357 onwards. According to the Rolls of Parliament (the official record), Hungerford *avait les paroles pur les communes d'Angleterre en cet parliament,* being broadly translated as 'spoke for the Commons of England in this Parliament."

Then and through 150 speakers during 650 years since, Mr Speaker has been above the political hurly-burly. He resigns from his political party, and may not re-join it even after he has given up the Speakership (viz those great speakers Betty Boothroyd, Bernard Weatherill and George Thomas of Tonypandy). He or she must 'speak' for every MP, upholding our rights and privileges. To do so he cannot and must not enter into any kind of political discussion or controversy – national or international. He has his own views, no doubt, about which he may chunter over the breakfast table, but he is simply not allowed to express them, nor let them be known in public. He is largely unopposed in his constituency at General Elections, and in every way, rather like the referee in a football match, must show neither 'fear nor favour.'

Most famously, Charles I was the last monarch to enter the Chamber of the House of Commons. (We chopped off his head as a result, and commemorate his exclusion every year at the State Opening of Parliament by banging our door in the face of the monarch's servant, Black Rod.) King Charles wanted to arrest five MPs who had meanwhile made good their escape down the Thames for alleged high treason. When the King asked Speaker Lenthall if he knew of their whereabouts, he replied: "May it please your Majesty, I have neither eyes to see nor tongue to speak in this place but as the House is pleased to direct me, whose servant I am here."

These conventions – together with such symbols as the mace on the Table in the House, the obscure and antiquated uniforms which the doorkeepers, Clerks at the Table and (until recently) Mr Speaker wear; the careful language, the rules of procedure together make our great Parliament what it is. Lose them and you lose the reputation of our parliamentary democracy. Every town council preserves its mayoral robes and chains of office, its clerks in wigs (every Caribbean democracy uses wigs, every dictatorship has abolished them). Coalminers' brass bands pride themselves on their uniforms; trades unions have their banners and sashes of office; Scottish clans love their tartan, the Highland Games Chieftains have their strict rules of dress and ancient rituals; beefeaters, guardsmen, the Queen and her Horseguards; the King's Troop firing their first world war guns as a salute to her 65th year since accession in Hyde Park. It's the very weft and weave of British history and tradition in all its glory, and we hack away at it at our peril.

The building comes into this too. The Palace of Westminster is iconic – in the real sense of that word. It symbolises all that is good about our parliamentary democracy. Do away with it, or alter it beyond recognition, modernise it or vulgarise it as you like, but by that action you will also be destroying its authority and stature around the world.

And in the meantime, unheeded by us, the government are allowed to get on with whatever they want to unhampered by our only mildly irritating scrutiny. It is a weak, idle and emasculated Parliament indeed.

"Throw away the even-handedness of the Speaker today; get rid of the clerks' wigs tomorrow; allow MPs to wear jeans and tee shirts the day after – you name it. Let's get rid of all these silly old traditions. Let's modernise for modernisation's sake."

State opening of Parliament.

Well if you do you are salami-slicing away at the whole basis of decent government and a universally respected Parliament. 'Modernisation' for modernisation's sake is meaningless. None of us have ever had a single constituent telling us how the clerks' wigs make Parliament distant and stuffy. (On the contrary, they love the ceremony and furbelows.) Vellum for our laws is taught to every school class as a symbol of how sacred they are; officials of all sorts wear their ancient traditional garb for the very simple reason that as they don it, they are by that very action suppressing their own personalities if favour of the rights and duties, the honour and distinction of their offices. They are no longer Mr Smith or Mr Brown; they are the Clerks at the Table and the Speaker in his chair. They are the very visible symbol of the ancient greatness which is our Parliament; and without them we are as nothing – as men of straw blowing in the wind.

Of course there are always some things which could do with improvement. The House of Lords is one of them.

David Cameron's Resignation Honours List in 2016, for example, caused a bit of a hoo-hah. And to a degree I understand and sympathise. Is it really a proper use of the honours system to thank people simply for doing their job – a job for which, no doubt, they were perfectly adequately paid? 'In this day and age' is there really still a role for handles – 'Sir this', 'Dame that', the 'Noble Baroness of somewhere or another', or is it all an outdated anachronism? Is it right to use membership of the House of Lords in particular in this way? If it's a legislature, should it really be a rest home for spin doctors and former MPs?

Well, my own view is that there is most definitely a role for titles to signify distinguished service to the country in one way or another. We like to be called 'Mr' or 'Ms' or 'Wing-Commander;' or 'His Worshipful the Mayor' and so on. These handles attached to one's name advertise one's role, one's distinction. I take greater pride in the letters 'MP' after my name than almost anything else, and would sooner change my name than lose those magic little letters (the privilege of using them of course being granted to me not by a grateful PM, but by the kind electors of North Wiltshire who have increased my majority in each of my six General Elections so far!)

I do, however, think, that we have to do something about the House of Lords. It currently has 681 Life Peers, 92 hereditaries (who are, bizarrely enough, the only ones actually elected to the House of Lords), 26 bishops, a total of 797, making it one of the largest legislative bodies in the world. (And bear in mind that there are only 350 seats in the Chamber! They must all be sitting on each other's knees.)

There are 243 Tories, 173 Crossbenchers, 209 Labour, 105 Liberal Democrats (who have only eight MPs in the Commons), the balance being bishops and various odds and sods. So the government do not have a majority and have as a result been defeated in the last year more often than in any other Parliament. The elected House is routinely being prevented from carrying out its perfectly manifesto-justified business by rather an odd bunch of peers. There is an ever-present risk, for example, that the unelected house, especially the disproportionately large number of Liberal Democrat peers, might seek to frustrate the Brexit process. That, of course, would be a constitutional outrage, which, if it were to occur, might well result in the significant reform, or even ultimately the abolition of the House of Lords. It would simply not be acceptable for a rag-bag of unelected Lords to frustrate the will of the people so clearly expressed in a Referendum and then translated into legislation by the elected government of the country. I suspect their Lordships know that they are playing with fire, and may well eventually back down. Precious few of them are kamikaze, and to be fair to them most are reasonably sensible supporters of the delicate UK Constitution, and the careful balance between the rights and privileges and duties of the two houses.

I am wholly opposed to an elected Lords, which might well set itself up in opposition to the elected House of Commons. So we need to find a way of pruning the Lords to a manageable size, and giving the government a greater expectation that they will get their business through. It is also wrong that peers' allowances, while at first glance generous, nonetheless mean that only those with some kind of outside income can afford to be in the Lords. That cannot be right. Is it not about time that we had a smaller working House of Lords, properly set up with secretaries and the like, and very probably salaried? Modest reform of that kind may well be long overdue.

Great as our Parliament is, and has been for the best part of 1000 years, there are worrying signs of its authority being undermined; its powers whittled away. So what do we need to do about it? First, we should, as we Conservatives always promised to do, abolish timetable motions. That might well make life less comfortable for we backbenchers. The parliamentary day would be less predictable. We might have to cancel some of our overseas trips, perhaps stay in Westminster for longer in the evening. It might well be a bit of a bore; but it's the job we signed up to. Until recently Thursday was a full sitting day with government business, quite often on Fridays too. Ours should be at least a four day a week Parliament, if not five days.

We should limit the worthy but perhaps relatively ineffectual Westminster Hall debates, Adjournment debates, Backbench Business Committee debates and Opposition Days. They give us the warm illusion of holding the government to account, but are in reality largely ignored.

We should limit the number of constituency staff, and seek to cut back on 'casework' which largely involves us in doing things which actually ought to be done by local councillors, social workers, immigration lawyers and so forth. Is it really right that HMG spends hundreds of millions of pounds a year enabling us to do things which are not truly part of our job descriptions, largely in order to ensure that we get re-elected? "He's a good Constituency MP" now tends to mean not that "he is representing Loamshire well by speaking up for us in Parliament", but that "he is always here." Do we represent Loamshire in Westminster, or Westminster in Loamshire? It is my view that the pendulum has swung too far towards the latter.

Perhaps it may be instructive to ask the most basic of all questions: "What's an MP for?"

In essence, we have seven core functions:
1. To make, amend, improve, or stop the making of laws
2. To examine the daily workings of the executive branch of government, and 'hold it to account.'
3. To represent the interests of our constituents in Westminster
4. To support our party or colleagues in a collective effort to govern or to oppose
5. To advance causes national or local in Parliament
6. To liaise with or scrutinise EU and devolved administrations
7. To carry out 'case-work' and constituency matters

Of them, you will have spotted that I have put 'constituency casework' at the bottom. Some will not agree. The newly elected whose priority is to establish themselves in the patch, or those with a small majority, will argue that 'casework' is their first priority and duty.

Yet is it really our job to deal with immigration appeals, benefits disputes, Child Support Agency arguments, planning applications, school placements and the like? Is there not a risk that it diverts us from our true purpose of running the country and holding the government to account?

It may be instructive that forty years ago there was a total of 25 secretaries in Parliament to look after all 630 MPs. Today there are 2700 members of staff. Doing what? And why? Is it really a proper use of parliamentary funds, for example, to have a team of three or four sitting in a High Street in one's constituency generating more and more case-work, rather than in Westminster helping us with our true parliamentary work?

It may well suit the agenda of the government very nicely. The more we do in our constituencies (and in harmless, if worthwhile, pursuits like backbench debates, all party groups and the like), the less we will trouble them.

How wrong all of this is. The complexity of government is certainly no less today than it has ever been. Legislation has in fact vastly increased in numbers in recent years, and vastly decreased in quality. Why? Because we are failing to scrutinise it properly in Parliament. Why? Because we don't have enough time to do so. Surely we should be seeking to extend parliamentary hours and scrutiny rather than shortening them?

There are other aspects of this, too. In opposition, the Conservatives opposed all Programme Motions. Yet in government – surprise, surprise – we are applying them just as enthusiastically as did Labour. Yet time is one of the very few weapons which Her Majesty's Loyal Opposition has at their disposal. It can hold bills up, keep government backbenchers in Westminster, spring surprises, ambush the government, and generally make life as difficult as it can for ministers. That is their proper role and all governments hate it.

They would be secretly content if backbenchers put them into power and then went quietly off into the night – little moles beavering away with our casework, emerging blinking into the sunlight just in time to ensure their re-election to power at the next General Election.

Is it not time to reverse this decline? To strengthen Parliament at the expense of the over-mighty executive, to re-establish our supremacy over institutions like the EU and devolved administrations? To energise the press and public's interest in and respect for the parliamentary process; and to correct the increasing belief that 'case-work' is what we are all here to do?

The collegiate nature of Parliament – 'the place where people speak' – should be enhanced, not diminished. Macmillan was of the view that of the 2000 rooms in the Palace, the young backbencher need only trouble himself with two – the

Chamber and the Smoking Room. Parliament works because people move around the building attending events, talking, swapping experiences, plotting. That would be destroyed at a stroke by 'family friendly hours.' And 'decanting' us elsewhere to make life easier for the vastly extravagant mending of the mechanical and electrical engineering systems which some people are proposing would end it for all time.

Cromwell, Disraeli, Churchill, Macmillan would not have allowed that. They believed in the power and supremacy not of government, but of Parliament. It is our inheritance and our duty to take radical steps to preserve and enhance that primacy.

Post-Brexit, many of the powers which we have lost to the EU over fifty years will be returned to the UK. We must ensure that they are not just hoovered up by the government; and that Parliament is the body which must decide how they are used and then keep a watchful eye on it. Brexit may be the moment, and the means, to reinvigorate Parliament.

Much has been made – during the campaign and since the Brexit decision – about the Scottish National Party, and whether or not they will in one way or another make use of the Brexit turmoil to demand a Second Referendum on Scottish independence. Similar, if less immediate, questions are asked about Northern Ireland (especially with regard to the 'open border' with the Schengen member, Eire), and Wales. Theresa May has been satisfactorily robust in batting away any such suggestion. "Now is not the time for these discussions," she has said." We will be negotiating to leave the EU as the UK. After all it is the UK as a whole who are members of the EU and only the UK as a whole may therefore leave it," is broadly her argument.

Yet counter-intuitively, I suspect that that answer may be exactly what the SNP and their charismatic (if you like that kind of thing) leader, Nicola Sturgeon, wants. She wants to demand such a referendum; she wants to campaign for an independent Scotland. Yet, especially with oil at around $50 a barrel, she knows perfectly well that an independent Scotland would economically simply not be able to stand on her own two feet. It is estimated that she would be running a deficit of £18 billion pa, which has eye-watering consequences for her economy. And the sensible and hard-headed people of Scotland know that perfectly well. What that means is that in her heart of hearts, Nicola Sturgeon really does not want a second referendum (which she would stand a good chance of losing with catastrophic political consequences for herself and her party). Nor does she want independence, which would result in a bankrupt Scotland. It would also very probably result in the end of the Scottish National Party and of Miss Sturgeon herself, in a directly analogous way to the destruction of UKIP post-Brexit. An independent Scotland would have no need for the Scottish National Party, and politics would very probably settle back into a much more traditional left versus right type of political debate. So the SNP do not want a referendum and they do not want independence.

What they want is to be able to campaign for both things; to argue that it is those heartless beasts in Westminster who are refusing to let them have it; and to blame the woes of the world on London, on the Tories, or on virtually anyone bar themselves. Campaigning like that puts them in an admirable position, and a position of considerable power. Actually achieving their goals would mean their own effective self-destruction.

So I do not believe for one second that Brexit will lead to the collapse of the United Kingdom. On the contrary, a strong and independent UK of Great Britain and Northern Ireland would be hugely attractive to the voters in all of the nations we have united over the centuries under one flag. After all, it was a Scottish King, James VI and I, who came South in 1603 to take over the English throne; and it was in 1707 that the Scots first realised how beneficial it would be to be part of the UK Parliament. Long may it last.

However, a continuing strong and united country and Parliament will be dependent on one further significant reform to the way we currently do business. William Hague brought in some weak, and virtually unworkable, procedural changes towards the end of his Commons career in a fairly half-hearted attempt to answer that question first posited by Tam Dalyell when he was MP for West Lothian – the eponymous 'West Lothian Question.'

In the last Scottish Independence Referendum, "Should Scotland be independent?" was the question. 1,617,989 thought she should; but 2,001,926 disagreed. It was a pretty resounding 55% plays 45% victory for the Unionists (a larger victory of course, than that enjoyed by the Brexit campaign only two years later). So that, surely, should be that?

Yet in the 2015 General Election, less than twelve months after that referendum, the 'Yes' voters , or at least most of them (1,454,456), voted SNP. As a result, the SNP secured just over 50% of the votes cast, and hardly surprisingly won 56 out of the 59 Scottish seats. Why none of the electoral pundits saw that coming is a mystery. In a first-past-the-post voting system, support from 50% of the electorate inevitably results in a landslide. After all, in the same General Election, the Tories formed a government nationally with only 37% of the votes cast. What had happened in Scotland, of course, was that the Unionist vote split three ways (Labour, Conservative and Lib Dem), while the nationalist vote held pretty steady and was given to only one party. Hardly rocket science.

The 2015 SNP landslide was dramatically reversed in the (otherwise catastrophic) Theresa May General Election in 2017. This time the Scot Nats secured 978,000 votes (down from 1.5 million), or 37% of the vote, and their seats at Westminster were reduced from 53 to 35. The Tories meanwhile secured 757,949 votes in Scotland (or 29%) , allowing them 13 MPs, their best result north of the Border since 1987, and even Labour and the Lib Dems were allowed a small improvement. Labour: 7 seats with 27%, Lib Dems 4 seats with 7.5%.

The SNP had paid the price of government (in Holyrood), of a general disaffection with some individuals (two of their MPs had been suspended suspected of corruption of one sort or another), and with a kind of general weariness with them. The result of the 2017 election ultimately may have been seen a bit of an unexpected decline for the Tories nationally, but it was a triumph in Scotland. And that secured two additional purposes. The result reconfirmed that the people of Scotland as a whole really do NOT want independence; and it knocked on the head the implicit threat from Brexit to the Union. The result effectively gave Theresa May a mandate to negotiate on behalf of the whole of the UK, and killed off any (pretty silly) suggestion of a separate Scottish negotiation or referendum.

Now despite my Scottish ancestry and upbringing, I gave up any part in Scottish politics many years ago, when I had the honour of being the shortest-lived ever Shadow Secretary of State for Scotland. Michael Howard (perfectly reasonably) fired me from the Shadow Cabinet after only six days on account of some untoward comments on BBC *Newsnight* about the effect that the Scottish Devolution Settlement was having on the people of England. My views then are now commonplace and a central part of Conservative policy. So my sole ambition in regard to Scottish politics today is to fight for the interests of the people of England, especially those of North Wiltshire who I am proud to represent.

The very existence of the Scottish Parliament, the so-called Devolution settlement in many ways militates against the interests of we English.

How can it be that Scottish MPs in Westminster, who have no say over health and education in Scotland can vote, ask questions and generally intervene in the running of the health and education systems in England? How can it be that a Scottish MP could be a minister in an English Department of State when the opposite cannot occur? How is it that Scottish MPs think it perfectly legitimate to interfere in English matters (English fox-hunting being perhaps the most iconic recent example), when of course the reverse is impossible. Why is it that the SNP are now the third party in Westminster with a right to respond to every debate, whether English, Scottish Welsh or Northern Irish? I was bemused to chair a Westminster Hall debate recently over road improvements in Suffolk, to be told that I had to call an SNP spokesman to wind up from the front bench. Over road improvements in Suffolk? How so?

There's an imbalance in the day-to-day role of an MP as well. In England, I have responsibility for every aspect of government. My surgeries and mailbag are stuffed full of people wanting to talk to me about education, about health, about transport, housing, local government and so much more. The Scottish MP at Westminster, by contrast, has no responsibility for those matters. Their Member of the Scottish Parliament (MSP) counterparts look after all of that. All that Scottish MPs at Westminster have responsibility for are non-devolved matters like Defence and Foreign affairs. Debates and question times in Parliament are predominantly English. Scottish MPs have a pretty easy time of it as a result, but of course they have the same salaries, rights and privileges as those of us who are full-blooded and comprehensive representatives of our electorate on every aspect of government.

What's more, the people of Scotland are heavily over-represented and over-politicised. There are now 59 Scottish MPs at Westminster plus 129 MSPs at Holyrood. So the 4 million voters in Scotland have a total of 188 MPs looking after them, or 21,276 voters per representative. The equivalent figure in England is 72,000, giving every Scottish voter 3.5 times more MPs than their English equivalent. Does that over-representation really make their lives better?

There's a problem with money, too. How can it be that, despite their right to make their own spending decisions, Scotland still enjoys – under the so-called Barnett Formula – a disproportionate level of Government spending? In the last year for which figures are available, HMG spent £8529 per head of the population in England, £10,152 per head of the population in Scotland. How can it nowadays be justified to spend £1623 per head more in Scotland than England? What it means effectively is that the people of North Wiltshire are cross-subsidising the people of Wick. Well, say I, why should they? The Scots have their own government. Let them raise their own taxes, pay for themselves, and face the political consequences if they get it all wrong.

All of these questions, first spotted by that late and great Labour MP, Tam Dalyell as the 'West Lothian Question', and many allied ones, were what troubled me during my brief spell as Shadow Secretary of State for Scotland. I was sacked for asking them. Yet they are the very questions which William Hague was tasked with finding an answer to in the immediate aftermath of the Scottish Independence Referendum in 2004. I fear that the solution he produced, which has been written into the Standing Orders of the House of Commons does not even come close to answering them. Lord Hague was tasked with creating a system of "English votes on English laws." Yet the end result is the fairly weak-kneed proposal that through a complex double-voting process written into the Standing Orders of the House, English MPs would have an effective veto over any Bill which has been certified by the Speaker to be purely English in its effect.

It's pretty feeble. SNP MPs can still vote on English laws; they can still vote on the English Budget. It has had no effect on Statutory Instruments; it does not prevent Scottish MPs being English ministers, nor Scottish MPs asking questions in English Departmental question times, nor speaking in purely English debates. It is a pretty transparent and altogether useless attempt to assuage English wrath over yet more powers being given to the Scottish Parliament. It simply will not achieve that. The people of England have still 'not spoken'. But they will do soon. We English are missing out, and we will not stand for it much longer.

So, let me propose a solution (first adumbrated by Lord [Michael] Forsyth) which would neatly answer quite a number of these unfair anomalies.

First, Scottish parliamentary boundaries should be redrawn to achieve parity with England. At 75,000 voters per seat, there would be 53 Scottish MPs rather than the current 59. Those MPs should serve in Holyrood to discuss purely

Scottish devolved matters, while we English MPs were simultaneously sitting in Westminster dealing with purely English matters. That could be, for example, on Mondays and Tuesdays, all of us then coming together in Westminster on Wednesdays and Thursdays to discuss UK wide issues. The same could of course apply to Wales and Northern Ireland.

There would be a straight first past the post voting system both north and south of the border, the party with the largest number of MPs forming the national government in each national parliament, which might of course be a different political party to that forming the overall UK Government. That is no different to the current situation, with an SNP Government in Scotland but a Conservative one nationally.

Such a semi-federal solution would reduce the overall cost of government; it would finally answer the West Lothian Question; it would reduce the over-representation and governance of the Scots. It would appeal to both English and Scottish voters; it would enhance the standing of Scottish MPs, by removing their current second-class status in Westminster.

It is radical. But it would reduce government, improve representation, and sort out what is at the moment a constitutional muddle.

Let's call it the North Wiltshire Answer to the West Lothian Question.

The Westminster parliamentary system has always had – and perhaps post-Brexit will have even more – of an influence on parliamentary democracies around the world. It is a flawed and often-changing system, which may above all be the best possible reason for our non-written constitution. Huge constitutional changes are made in Britain by a majority in both Lords and Commons. The introduction of the Welsh and Scottish Parliaments, possible changes to our voting system (which was then dismissed in a referendum), the whole question of Brexit itself, was decided by a simple majority of MPs and peers. What a contrast there is in that to, for example, then US system. The American Constitution was designed to counter-balance an over mighty monarch by establishing a complex series of checks and balances which effectively mean that no single institution can do anything without the approval of the others. Constitutional change, in particular, is virtually impossible, and there is frequent legislative and executive 'grid-lock' amongst the two Houses on Capitol Hill and the White House.

Our age-old – and perhaps in detail flawed – parliamentary system has a great deal to offer the world. Our new-found parliamentary freedom post-Brexit will hugely enlarge and enhance that capability. Ours will once again become the Mother of Parliaments throughout the developed and developing world. Brexit could well be just the stimulus our somewhat diminished Parliament needs.

16. Britain: An Intellectual Power House

"The Bloomsbury highbrow, with his mechanical snigger, is as out-of-date as the cavalry colonel. A modern nation cannot afford either of them."
(George Orwell: *England your England*)

None of the things we are seeking for the post-Brexit Britain – trade, aid, warfare, governance, business, or the rest of it, can be done without sheer intellectual power. It was our education, universities in particular, and ability to think in general, which powered the Industrial Revolution, and thereby created the greatest empire the world has ever known. And we can only ever aspire to that kind of greatness again in this post-Brexit world if we can once again dominate the world's brain-waves.

Our great education system could best be described as 'hybrid'. Most people (8.2 million pupils all told) go to one of our 24,372 schools in the UK (including nursery schools, primary and secondary schools, special schools and independent schools). There is one in easy walking distance of every house in the country. Where else can readily boast that? (And, of course, many parts of the world have no such schools at all, far less geographically handy ones.) Classes of 30 or fewer would be viewed as a great luxury in many parts of the world, and would have been viewed as a luxury in my own primary school, Glasgow's Hillhead School, where the average in my day was around 40.

Not only do we have plenty of them, but by and large, and certainly by comparison with other countries, their general standard of education is overall outstanding. There have been changes in recent years with most becoming self-governing 'Academies.' Intelligent human-beings, whether they be in business, education or local government are the people best paced to make decisions about their own institutions, and Academy status allows just that. A minimum of interference and bossiness which must be the ambition of any worthwhile libertarian government is well exemplified in academies. They balance their books, employ their own staff, and decide on a great many academic matters. And the quality of education offered as a result well demonstrates the excellence of the system.

Within that total are 163 grammar schools teaching 170,000 children. They cause more angst than almost any other part of our education system. Yet why should it be that we tend to resent people who are academically more able than we are? Not everyone is good at essays, advanced mathematics, Latin and history. Surely it is only right that we should encourage them, give them every possible help and assistance, allow them to rise to the top of their academic careers without any resentment or envy. Just as we admire the Olympic athletes, praise those who can do all sorts of things that we ourselves cannot or would not want to do; is it not right that we should admire and praise and help those who are more academically able or ambitious than we are?

People are happy to give out athletes all sorts of special – elitist – training. But we cavil at special – elitist – academic training. Why should that be the case? That is why I have always been a fan of grammar schools. My own school, Glasgow High School was academically excellent; but it was pretty lacking in practical skills, which is one reason for my own practical incompetence. I and people like me were 'good at our books'. The High School was socially inclusive – kids from all over Glasgow and from every background went there if they were of an academic frame of mind. The Socialists tried to close it down in the 'sixties; it became a private school and so now is academically excellent but also socially exclusive. Well done, Socialists, you have deprived some of the poorest people in Glasgow of some of the best education they could get – and entirely free of charge. Selection should be about merit, not ability to pay.

The best in education should be enabling ALL to achieve their potential – in music, arts, academia, technical apprenticeships. Working out who is good at what (selection) is a very necessary part of it. Let us help and encourage excellence in academics, just as we do in sport or in practical capabilities.

That some people are good at some things, others at others is acknowledged in the grammar school system, and in rigorous setting in comprehensives. Grammar Schools without doubt forced the intellectual excellence of the twentieth century, and they could do again, although it can reasonably be argued against by the 'sheep and goats' nature of the Eleven Plus examinations and the second-best feeling about Secondary Modern Schools as a result. But it seems to me obvious that selection, streaming, specialisms, call it what you will, is an essential part of truly successful education. The 'sixties version of comprehensive education – under which every child, of whichever ability and whichever curriculum bent was taught the same stuff in the same way in the same classroom, was an educational product of Communist egalitarianism. Like Communism, it failed. It produced the lowest common denominator of product, and stagnation, and second ratedness was the inevitable consequence. Students all have something to offer. A worthwhile education system must have methods of deciding what that is – academic, scientific, business, practical – and then providing the best education and training to nurture and bring on that ability or tendency. And that, by definition, means some form of selection or streaming.

The Scottish system of education has always been held out as one of the greatest educational assets of the UK. A glance at the educational background of so many of the 'great and the good' listed, for example in Who's Who, proves that to be the case today as in the heyday of empire – providing breadth of education through the 'Highers' system, followed by four-year honours degrees at Scottish universities as opposed to the depth provided by the English A Level system, which of course is followed by a three-year undergraduate degree.

Then there are 2500 independent schools in the UK today, educating some 615,000 students. That is 7% of the total, but rising to 18% of the over sixteen year olds. The clearest possible evidence of their excellence must come from the number of foreign parents, especially the Chinese and Russians, who choose – at huge inconvenience and expense – to send their children to English boarding schools. Fully 15% of the students at Eton and Wellington, for example, are from overseas (doubled in twenty years). At Brighton College, 9.7% of students are from overseas, 5.5% from Hong Kong, with others coming from countries as diverse as Russia, Bulgaria, China and Oman. At Malvern St James's School, 30% of pupils are foreign, but it may be a sign of times to come that only 46% of new entrants are British. At present 21% of all non-British pupils are from China, 18% from Hong Kong, 10% from Russia, 7% from Germany, 5% from Spain and 4.3% from Nigeria. In total there are 27,200 foreign pupils in British private schools, and a further 16,800 foreign students whose parents live in the UK. The reality is that with fees running at £30,000 pa (or £60,000 pa from pre-tax income), these schools are frankly beyond the reach of any middle-income families.

The excellence (and popularity) of British private school education is further evidenced by the number of institutions which have set up 'daughter' schools overseas. Harrow led by opening a branch in Thailand in 1998, and then Harrow International in Beijing in 2005, and one is planned shortly for Hong Kong. Sherborne is opening a branch in Qatar, and long-established is St George's British International School in Rome, and Dulwich College, Shanghai, which is soon to be followed by two other Dulwich Chinese branches. Repton has opened a school in Dubai; Haileybury has just opened a branch in Almaty, Kazakstan; and quite leaving aside British schools with branches overseas, some 2000 schools worldwide claim to offer a British curriculum. And it's not only private schools. The City Academy in Bristol is said to be currently exploring the possibility of branches in the Democratic Republic of the Congo and Zimbabwe.

Of course it's not only academic prowess which is offered by English private schools. Our medal success in the 2012 Olympics in London and 2016 in Rio, for example, is not about education provided by the state, as it most certainly is in China and America. We should not be ashamed of, but rejoice in, the fine medals performance by those (unlike me) lucky enough to have enjoyed an English public school education. Around 28% of Team GB at Rio was privately educated (including six from Millfield alone), with 33% of the medal winners being from private schools, rising to 50% in some sports such as rowing. Our private schools have always been one home of great British sporting prowess, which may be one reason why they are becoming the envy of the world. It must be one of the greatest ironies of modern times that 21% of overseas pupils in our public schools and 90,000 in our universities come from Communist China. It would be good to know how many of the Chinese Olympic medallists had in fact been educated in an English private school. (Their solitary equestrian eventer in 2012, for example, was an Etonian!)

There are many elements, many strands to our intellectual dominance – the playing fields of Eton are an oft-cited source of our industrial and imperial greatness, and it is without doubt true that our great English Public Schools, so farsightedly founded in the main part by our Tudor forebears played a huge part in the Engine house of our greatness.

We used to be proud that the empire had been built on the playing fields of Eton. Now we politicians disguise our predominantly public school and Oxbridge Cabinet with falsely estuarial whines in our voices and cringe with embarrassment every time that famous Bullingdon Club photograph of David Cameron and Boris Johnson reappears. I salute Jacob Rees-Mogg who suffers from no such inverted snobbery, and whose magnificent put-down of David Dimbleby on the *Question Time* programme goes down as one of the greats. "Something to do with your Eton education?" sneered Dimbleby. "Yes", replied Jacob without a hair stirring," I was there with your son". Part of the universal admiration for the Mogg comes from his absolute refusal to play down his very privileged background. That is admired by people from all strata in society. Perhaps one of the lessons of the Olympics should be that we thank and congratulate and take pride in our public schools, and then see what we can do to our State system of education to try to emulate them. A good place to start would be to do away with egalitarianism and re-invent that harsh reality of real life – that there are winners and losers in sport as in academia.

And British Educational Greatness is not, of course, just about the playing fields of Eton.

The fact is that warts and all the totality of the British system of school education is overall extremely good. It's easy to knock it. Every parent whose child muffs his exams blames the school system; very rarely their muddled headed children, or even less likely their

Eton Wall Game.

©Spottswood (cc3.0)

unhelpful home background. We Brits love to knock what is great. Yet the truth is that our education system really is second to none in the world. It was that which made Britain great in the nineteenth century and it can do so again.

Our Universities too are second to none in the world, boasting four in the top ten (Oxford, Cambridge, University College London and Imperial College, London), beaten only by America claiming five and Switzerland the tenth. The Russell Group of Universities (Birmingham, Bristol, Cambridge, Cardiff,

Durham, Edinburgh, Exeter, Glasgow, Imperial College London, King's College London, Leeds, Liverpool, London School of Economics, Manchester, Newcastle, Nottingham, Oxford, Queen Mary College, London, Queen's University Belfast, Sheffield, Southampton, University College London, Warwick and York) offer a solid base of excellence in tertiary education, offering more than half a million students an outstanding educational experience and world-renowned degree qualification. The UK is a European intellectual and academic powerhouse and always has been.

But it's not just education for education's sake (although true traditionalists might rather wish it were). My first university (Glasgow) had the great advantage of being on a hill (Gilmorehill) in the centre of Glasgow. On one side lay the docks and shipbuilding yards, easily seen from one of the greatest engineering faculties in the world. Glasgow's Great Western Infirmary was a stone's throw from the world-beating medical department, the business area was just down the road. Education at Glasgow University was in a physical and very visible sense linked to the ultimate destination of the students. Not for us the 'dreaming spires' with our heads in the intellectual clouds.

Our age-old intellectual prowess as a nation is well-evidenced in the end result. We gave our language to the world, and have of course the greatest English literature, (leaving aside a few great Americans, for the moment, and always remembering that they nonetheless wrote in our English mother tongue!). Then our magazines and newspapers (who could better the *Times* and *Telegraph*, the *Economist* and *Spectator* – and to be even-handed the *New Statesman* and *Guardian*, whose journalism and writing is outstanding even if a bit 'lefty' for my personal taste. Our think-tanks (RUSI, Chatham House, IISS), our music (Elgar, Handel – German but writing most of his great works in England) artists (Stubbs and Constable) designers (Westwood and McQueen) and inventors (telephone, Oxygen, photography, TV, penicillin, the WorldWide Web and so much more) – are all evidence of the outstanding excellence of our education system and our global intellectual powers.

Yet we are modest about our intellectual achievements in a way which must astonish the rest of the world. Surely it is time that we recognised our intellectual, training, academic excellence – and eliteness in the world. Surely it is time that we became proud of what we have – as our ancestors were rightly proud of the Scottish system as of Eton – and that we started to recognise that it gives us the true ability to make a huge contribution to the world.

We have the schools and universities, we have the intellectual genes and chromosomes second to none on the world. We should be capitalising on that intellectual prowess with a view to running – or at least contributing to the running – of the world. We should be forcing our children to their best efforts, rather as the Japanese so successfully do, and we should be ready to give them proper adulation when they do well, and encouragement even when they do less well.

Britain is truly the intellectual powerhouse of the world. Let us recognise that, be proud of it, drive it forward and make it an absolutely central part of our new post-Brexit Britain.

17. Britain: A Public / Private Provider

"There is no such thing as Society." (Margaret Thatcher)

Britain leads the world in the provision of public services too. "There is no such thing as society," as Margaret Thatcher so famously said to *Women's Own* magazine in 1987. *"I think we've been through a period where too many people have been given to understand that if they have a problem, it's the government's job to cope with it,"* she continued. *"'I have a problem, I'll get a grant. I'm homeless, the government must house me.' They're casting their problem on society. And, you know, there is no such thing as society. There are individual men and women, and there are families. And no government can do anything except through people, and people must look to themselves first. It's our duty to look after ourselves and then, also to look after our neighbour. People have got the entitlements too much in mind, without the obligations. There's no such thing as entitlement, unless someone has first met an obligation."*

She was, perhaps unconsciously, (mis-)quoting W. H. Auden:

"There is no such thing as the State And no-one exists alone; ... We must love one another or die."

Many years later, David Cameron, by contrast, said *"There is such a thing as society, it's just not the same thing as the state."* His plan to complement the Thatcher economic revolution with a social one was overtaken by the 2008 financial crisis — and his "Big Society" mantra bombed at the 2010 election.

By the time we come to Theresa May, writing in the *Telegraph* after the Brexit Referendum, she is talking about something called a 'Shared Society':

"Overcoming these divisions and bringing our country together is the central challenge of our time.

That means building the shared society. A society that doesn't just value our individual rights but focuses rather more on the responsibilities we have to one another; a society that respects the bonds of family, community, citizenship and strong institutions that we share as a union of people and nations; a society with a commitment to fairness at its heart.

This must be the cause that animates us — the end towards which we work as we leave the EU and make the most of the opportunities ahead. It is the right response to those who voted for change back in June. And it goes to the heart of my belief that there is more to life than individualism and self-interest. The social and cultural unions represented by families, communities, towns, cities, counties and nations are the things that define us and make us strong.

And it is the job of government to encourage and nurture these relationships and institu-

tions where it can, and to correct the injustice and unfairness that divides us wherever it is found."

Questions and debates about the nature – and extent – of the state, or of society are as old as the state itself. The English Civil War, for example, in the Seventeenth Century, was all about how much power the King should have and how much the Parliament. At its simplest, Marxism was of the view that the state was all; that the individual was nothing by comparison (Stalin: *"The death of one man is a tragedy; the death of a million is a statistic"*). Citizens gave up their right to freedom in return for state supplied housing, education, holidays. Without the State there was nothing. It's a very extreme form, nay a perversion of the Social Contract of Hobbes, Locke and Hume. Their view was that the citizen voluntarily gives up certain freedoms in return for collective security and services. That is the very bedrock of civilised democratic institutions.

George Orwell's two great works, *1984* and *Animal Farm* may have been written seventy years ago, but their message is as fresh today as it was then.

"Do not imagine, comrades, that leadership is a pleasure! ... No one believes more firmly than Comrade Napoleon that all animals are equal. He would be only too happy to let you make your decisions for yourselves. But sometimes you might make the wrong decisions, comrades, and then where should we be?" (Animal Farm)

"The Party seeks power entirely for its own sake. We are not interested in the good of others; we are interested solely in power, pure power. ... Power is not a means; it is an end. One does not establish a dictatorship in order to safeguard a revolution; one makes the revolution in order to establish the dictatorship. The object of persecution is persecution. The object of torture is torture. The object of power is power." (1984)

Hyperbole and exaggeration both books may be, but there is a lesson in both for all of us concerned about the nature of the state or of society.

True, Thatcherism was probably the antithesis both of State Communism and misplaced 'caring' Socialist or Liberal interventionism. Socialists believe that the state should look after you; Thatcherite minimalist libertarians believe that the state should look after only those totally incapable of looking after themselves, which should be the duty of most of us. That enabled true believers to long for a time when the state could be abolished, when the market was the sole provider of all the citizen needed. State housing, education, road provision should all be abolished, and replaced by privatised provision. Thatcher did of course undertake something of a revolution is this regard, privatising most of the great national industries, from water and electricity to car parking and freight carriage; from the national airlines, to large parts of the heavily regulated banking system. She sold off large parts of the nation's housing stock to the tenants, gave tax relief to those who wanted private healthcare, and subsidised through tax reliefs private mortgages. The more extreme of her disciples would yearn for the virtual abolition of taxation, of voucher systems to make all education privately provided, and to hand the universal benefits system over to charitable providers.

Progressive privatisation of services provided by the state was brought to a pretty abrupt end both by internal political changes in the UK, and by increasing and centralising powers of the EU. It is not too fanciful to draw some parallels between the EU, and some aspects of Stalinist Russia. The Common Agricultural Policy in its earlier forms at least, bore a striking similarity to Communal farming. Farmers were paid huge subsidies not because their produce was needed, but because it was deemed helpful from a social standpoint to keep them in business. (Remember wine lakes, and grain and butter mountains?) To this day large amounts of EU subsidy goes to tobacco farmers in Italy and elsewhere, for largely social reasons, despite the fact that simultaneously the EU are campaigning to lower dependence on tobacco, and national governments are spending a fortune on dealing with the medical end product of smoking tobacco.

The reality is that both extreme views of the role of the state are forlorn, a reality towards which both Cameron and May were stumbling. The state/society has to do some things. The defence of the realm is a good example. No-one else will do that, nor the provision of policing and law and order and prisons. Care for those who cannot look after themselves – the sick, disabled, aged, mentally disabled must at least to some degree be the duty of the state, if no-one else will take on that responsibility. But total care from cradle to grave of the kind which Bevan promised and which we broadly currently enjoy in the UK is in all reality unaffordable, and will have to change. (Although it will be a brave politician indeed, and very probably a short-lived one, who proposes any kind of even modest privatisation of our beloved National Health Service, or perhaps a charitable-isation of parts of our overweening benefits system.)

The fact of the matter is that already, and increasingly over the next hundred years of artificial intelligence and robots, fewer and fewer of us are working to produce wealth, more and more of us are consuming it. That means that some form of rationing of long-term care for the elderly and healthcare must sooner or later have to happen.

I have a good friend in Chippenham, Miss Kitty Sparkes, whose fitness and brightness belies her 104 years of age. Every time I see her, Kitty is as sharp as a razor, quizzing me about all sorts of political and current events. She strolls into town most days to get her shopping, and is a regular attender at the local Conservative Ladies Luncheon Club. She was a midwife in the East End of London during the Blitz, when since there were no tin hats available they used upturned pots and pans. A lifetime of helping people, commitment to the community (and a love of jigsaws) has kept Kitty fit and healthy.

I was touched as I came down the stairs in Chippenham Station one evening by a tiny child – less than two years old I would think – in her mother's arms, but holding out her little hands and mouthing "Daddy" to the man on the stairs behind me. She has all of her life ahead of her. But for now, what mattered was her daddy coming home from work. That was her whole world, and all was now well in it. Kitty Sparks has so much to look back on and remember over 100 years. Yet she also has so much to look forward to. Every day has its adventures and its rewards.

If the little child in the station, or the two newly baptised babies on Kitty's knee at St Andrew's church the previous Sunday live to be 100 (which is nowadays increasingly likely), they will be able to say "I knew a lady who was born two hundred years ago." It's like us knowing someone who was born shortly after Waterloo. Not bad going.

Admire people like Kitty as we do, the statistics indicate that more and more of us will follow her example and achieve our centenary. In 1917, a year after Kitty was born, King George V started the tradition of sending out 100th birthday telegrams. He sent 24 cards that year. Since the beginning of her reign, the Queen has so far sent 110,000 birthday greetings. And in 25 years' time it is estimated that the monarch will be sending 250 such cards per day, or 100,000 every year. 550,000 Britons are now aged ninety or more (compared to 190,000 in 1984), and life expectancy for all of us has risen dramatically in recent years.

So is it really any surprise that our beloved NHS, committed to providing the best of healthcare from cradle to grave, is creaking a bit at the seams? The NHS employs 1.7 million people (making it the fifth largest employer in the world, and by far the largest in the UK), delivers services at over 7000 sites, costs £121 billion a year (£2000 per head of the population); and deals with 1 million patients every thirty-six hours, (85% of whom are thoroughly pleased with their treatment), including 10 million operations (up from 7 million in 2005), and 16 million hospital admissions, 28% more than a decade ago.

The fact is that as we live longer and longer, and have higher and higher expectations with regard to healthcare, it becomes less and less affordable. The government has increased spending on the NHS by more than inflation; but the costs are sky-rocketing. And developments in medical science mean that this trend will become worse and worse over the next twenty years unless we do something pretty radical about it.

There are cleverer minds than mine tussling with this huge problem. But here are a few ideas for them. The only important thing about our NHS is that it is excellent and that it is free. The way in which that is achieved should not really matter to us. So, for example, does the government really need to own all 7000 sites? Could we make better use of the private sector in one way or another? Are there ways to save money? For example, I was astonished when I visited my excellent GP's surgery in Yatton Keynell to collect my regular repeat prescription (painkillers for a minor affliction) a few days after my sixtieth birthday. "No charge", said the nice pharmacist, "now that you have turned sixty". But why should it be? My income is the same as it was when I was fifty-nine. Between July and November 2016, more than 31,000 GP, nurse and healthcare assistant appointments were missed across Wiltshire's 55 GP Practices – the equivalent of over 1033 days of general practitioner time. In Wiltshire, this boils down to a potential 6000 patients missing out on an opportunity to be seen each month.

It's no use using health as some kind of political football. Nor is spending more and more necessarily the right answer. We could spend the whole of the national wealth on it and it would still not be enough. No. As a society, we need to get together and quietly and reasonably work out how we can provide outstandingly world-renowned excellence in our healthcare, but do so in a way which is afford-able to the nation in the 100 years that lie ahead. We can't go on as we are, so let's get that Great British brain to work on the problem, and come up with a long-term solution, not just short-term sound bytes.

In days of yore we worked until we were sixty-five years of age, and died a couple of years later at sixty-seven/seventy. Today we have thirty years or more of retirement to look forward to. Not only that, but whereas in days of yore our bodies were allowed to age gracefully, our teeth fell out and our eyesight failed; when we were allowed to go 'mildly gaga' and get looked after by our tolerant families as a result, today we demand (perfectly reasonably) the absolute best that medical science can offer.

A 104-year old lady recently benefited from a hip replacement operation. More and more drugs capable of providing (or extending at least) lifestyle cost millions, often offering only a small betterment of the condition; or a week or two's extra life.

Sooner or later we will have to realise that universal benefits and healthcare and long-term care simply cannot be afforded. There is now – and will be a recurring imbalance between Bevan's aspiration for 'care from cradle to grave'; and what we can actually afford to provide free of charge. So what are we to do about it?

The first two options involve the rich providing for the poor. It would – at least in theory – be possible to increase the level of taxation (or the tax take, which is not necessarily the same thing) to a level which would pay for all of the medical and care needs the entire population could possibly want. Those rather self-right-eous people, the Liberal Democrats, often talk about 'putting a penny on income tax to pay for the NHS' as if somehow or another that would be a magic wand solution for now and for all time. It is of course no real solution – just a tooth-achingly self-righteous attempt at self-deprivation for the good of the whole. There is in reality nothing at all to say that 1% on income tax (which would raise at best about £5 billion) bears any resemblance to the current NHS shortfall (of perhaps £20 billion) nor that it would cover ongoing shortfalls in the future. For the reality is that no matter how much we taxed and spent it would still never be quite enough. And the more we tax the less likelihood is there that people will actually want to work hard to produce the wealth. The Laffer Curve shows that the higher the rate of tax, the less you collect and vice-versa. It's not about taxa-tion. A low-tax society in which people are truly motivated to work hard and to use their initiative and intelligence must be a pre-requisite of any self-sustain-ing society.

It's not about tax, but it is about spending better. There is currently vast wastage in every aspect of British public service provision – health, education, benefits, transport. It is also surely the case that those of us who can afford it should start to pay for more of the services we receive from the state. In healthcare, is there not some logic in extending the principle of contributing to costs for eye and dentistry, to GPs' surgery visits perhaps, to needless appearances at hospital Accident and Emergency units, perhaps ultimately to various other aspects of medical care. And before I am accused of "privatising the NHS", can I just point out that large parts of it are already and always have been in private hands. Dentists' surgeries, for example, are private property; pharmaceuticals, buildings, cleaning and catering are all private; so is the manufacture of beds and hospital equipment. Vast swathes of NHS spending go to the private sector already. Quite right too.

So will asking a few of us to pay just a little more really amount to a fundamental destruction of that holy cow the NHS – free to all at the point of delivery? And is asking the middle classes to pay their own way not vastly preferable to the unsustainable taxation solution?

If we cannot (and must not) pay for our public services by increased taxation or government borrowing (which is effectively the same thing), and if no amount of cost-cutting, waste management and efficiency saving will quite match our spending expectations; if charitable and philanthropic sources help, but are not enough; then what are we to do about it?

The answer, I think, comes from a fundamental change of approach. A marked toughening up of our thinking about the 'cradle to grave'. Do we really want our bodies patched up so that we easily reach 100 years of age? Do we really have to provide benefits for all no matter how long (or how hard) they have worked to contribute to society before they fell into need? Do we really need such vast expenditure on Health and Safety, or would we not be better to accept a higher degree of risk in our lives – in our factories, school visits and streets alike? Risk means that we accept some things happening which under other circumstances we would much rather we had avoided. A risk-aware, litigation-bound society is also a society which does not do anything. It is a hidebound society. The great entrepreneurs took risks; the explorers, the colonialists. Anything that is ever worthwhile involves risk.

There's nothing quite as risky as just being alive. I love those signs on pylons which read "Danger of Death." That's the problem with being born – we all suffer from a danger of death at some stage or another. Life is full of greater or smaller risks, yet if we don't take them we risk never leading life to the full. 'Speculate to accumulate' is the old City maxim – the more you risk in life, the more you are likely to benefit from it.

My friend, Swindon boy Sir David Hempleman-Adams has taken every risk

Sir David Hempleman-Adams.

there is in the book – Everest, the Poles, every ballooning record that exists. People like David or like British national Chris Norman and the three American off-duty soldiers who wrestled a terrorist gunman on Eurostar to the floor and disarmed him take risks (albeit carefully calculated ones); and we admire them greatly for it.

The Hawker Hunter pilot in the Shoreham Air Show took an ultimately tragic risk, and our hearts go out to the friends and families of those who were so sadly killed as a result. I suppose it is right and proper that the Civil Aviation Authority should have some very searching questions to ask about the causes of the tragedy, and some stringent regulation to put in pace to try to ensure that nothing like it ever happens again.

Yet I sometimes wonder if we are becoming a bit too risk averse as a nation. Are we giving up too much that is 'good' in favour of that which is 'safe'? Did you see that our friends in the EU are asking us to put up notices on Devon beaches to point out to the unwary that 'donkey rides can be dangerous'? An entirely risk-free life (if there were such a thing) would also be pretty dull. Thespians traditionally avoid wishing each other 'Good Luck' as they go on stage. Instead they say "Break a Leg" in the hope that their pessimism may be proved unnecessary, and actually work as a positive talisman.

The new EU-regulation free Britain must be ready to embrace risk, to realise that the world is a dangerous, perhaps an unpleasant place. And then to use our ingenuity and skills and wit not to avoid the risks and unpleasantness but to turn them to our advantage.

The British way must be for there to be a safe and secure safety net for those who simply cannot look after themselves, but for that safety net to be reasonably close to the ground.

18. Britain's Green and Pleasant Land

"Oh, to be in England now that April's there. And whoever wakes in England sees, some morning unaware, that the lowest boughs and the brushwood sheaf round the elm-tree bole are in tiny leaf, while the chaffinch sings on the orchard bough. In England – now."
Browning's immortal words crystallize the Englishman's relationship with the countryside.

Despite the fact that very few of us live there, and even fewer work on the land, we Brits love the countryside. In France, the more successful you are, the more you move towards the centre of towns and cities. The countryside and rural villages are consigned to the peasantry and to the eccentric English who seem to want to spend huge amounts of money buying uninhabitable French hovels. In England, by contrast, the more successful you are the further out you move - first to suburbia, then to a country village or town, ultimately for the very few, to the farm or Cotswold Manor House surrounded by a few thousand rolling acres.

We mainly live in towns yet we love the countryside and protect it fiercely. Our houses look out over the bypass to the green fields beyond thereby allowing us to think that we live in the countryside; and if we are meeting friends at the weekend what could be better than 'a little pub I know out in the country near here'? The Campaign for the Protection of Rural England, the Countryside Alliance, RSPB, National Trust – all are thriving, all symptomatic of our rather romantic love affair with rural Britain.

Yet despite all of that, we really have very little clue about farming, and the brutalities of life in the country. Badgers and foxes are cuddly and wise, no matter what damage they may do to cows and chickens respectively. Deer are baby Bambis, wholly ignoring the wholesale destruction of valuable crops which they may wreak. 28,000 cows are slaughtered every year because of the drive to eradicate badger-borne Bovine TB; yet a few badgers humanely destroyed (and by that means themselves spared a horrible death from TB deep inside their sett) causes outcry amongst some, and at very least an uneasy feeling amongst most of us no matter how committed we are to the cull. We are blind to the fate of hedgehogs and bumble bees, which are always notably absent from an area inhabited by a large number of badgers, having been ritually slaughtered by that most efficient of killers, Bertie Brock the wise old badger. Anyone who has seen the devastation a fox can wreak in a chicken run for no reason but the satisfaction of killing

Bratton White Horse, Wiltshire.

chickens, whose carcasses they very often leave lying around, would happily throttle the stinking vermin which Basil Brush in reality is. Yet we love foxes and badgers and would rather throttle the farmer who would kill them to safeguard their own livelihood.

We have really very little clue about the link between Easter lambs frolicking in the lush green pastures and our Sunday roast; our stomachs would turn at everyday sights in the abattoir. We urban Brits are thoroughly soppy about animals. And we are astonishingly unsympathetic to farmers despite their magnificent role as guardians of the landscapes we love, and providers of the high quality and affordable food on our tables which we demand.

Just as there is a curious disconnect between our love for the 'brave boys and girls' in our armed forces and a hatred of what they have to do on active service overseas; so there is a particularly schizophrenic disconnect between our love of the countryside and its produce, yet our mild (or worse) disapproval of what farmers have to do to achieve it.

Throughout the EU Referendum Campaign there was talk (much of it apocalyptic) about the effect which leaving the EU would have on British farming. It would be 'the end of farming as we know it' we were told. Instead of the CAP comfort blanket with guaranteed acreage subsidies to farmers, guaranteed by those dozy individuals in Brussels, we would have our own MPs in Westminster deciding how/whether/if farmers should get anything at all. "What if we have a Labour government and they give all the money to schools and hospitals?" was the regular question.

While to an extent human preference for the known and comfortable is always understandable, there are three obvious flaws with that concern.

First, few farmers would argue that life has been absolutely brilliant under the CAP for the last fifty years. As a rural MP, I have spent twenty years fielding very genuine concerns and complaints. So where does this new-found nostalgia for the EU and CAP come from? We make a net contribution of £2 billion to the CAP, which we have to presume will come back to farming in the UK once we stop cross-subsidising loss-making small holdings on the Continent of Europe. After all, the British farmer currently gets disproportionately less than his European counterpart from the CAP (220 Euros per hectare, whilst the Belgian and Dutch farmer gets 460 Euros per hectare). EU countries view the CAP payments to farmers less as a means of producing good cheap food and more as a form of social security. That has cost British farmers (and consumers) a fortune over the years, and surely it is high time that that money was repatriated to the UK. Not only that but many EU inspired regulations, like the three-crop rule, for example, are regularly blamed by British farmers for so much that ails them

Second, there is no reasonable presumption that a government of any colour would simply cut funding off from farming resulting in its annihilation. It would be electoral suicide to allow our countryside to return to a wasteland, insisting that our shoppers should rely entirely on cheap imports from overseas instead. The UK voter, even if they live in towns, love the countryside and respect farmers as the guardians of it. And there is no real evidence that farmers have done much worse under Labour governments than Conservative ones. (Indeed I have an instinctive suspicion that the opposite may be the case. And at all events, if any interest group fears what a Labour government would do, then they have an obvious remedy to their fears at the ballot box.)

And third, is it not quite wrong to abdicate responsibility for decisions which should be made by our own elected representatives to a faceless group of quangocrats overseas in the hope that their decisions might somehow or another be better than our own? If that is the case, then it highlights all that is wrong with the EU – that it is somehow or another supranational – protecting British citizens from our own worst excesses.

The current government has promised to maintain the current levels of subsidy until the next election in 2022 (they cannot constitutionally promise beyond that date, since it will be a new Parliament, at least theoretically possibly of a different political hue).

There is every reason to presume that the British government will continue to subsidise farming to a similar level as at present, both because our rural-loving electorate will demand it, and because our farmers will need a similar level of subsidy to their competitors on the Continent of Europe and elsewhere if they are to remain in business. It seems to me likely that while the level will be comparable, the means of its distribution may well change. Production subsidy – paying people to produce things which would not otherwise be needed, which resulted in the butter mountains of old, has been replaced in more recent years in the CAP by a largely acreage-based subsidy. The more land you own the more cash you get. Yet there is a perversity about that too. Why should it be that an Arab Sheikh who happens to own x thousands of acres should be paid £y million simply because of that ownership. He may be a terrible landlord; he may conform to only the most basic of environmental rules and regulations, he may perversely be leaving the land to waste; yet he gets paid a fortune simply by virtue of that ownership. Surely those people are big enough to stand on their own two feet.

Should we not rather be using the government subsidy which will replace the CAP to pay for 'public goods'? Should it not pay for the environmental benefits we all want, for better access to the countryside perhaps, for the maintenance of our beloved landscapes, and perhaps to cross-subsidise the small family farmers, and those toiling over land which would not otherwise be economically cultivable – in our uplands and 'less favoured areas'? If a farmer is to leave his headlands and woodland uncultivated to encourage wild flowers, butterflies, bees and the rest of it, he will have to be compensated for it. Someone will need to pay for the foot-paths, bridges, bridleways, long-distance walking routes which we love. If we want small family farms producing local produce, often killed in small local abattoirs, then we will have to pay for it. If we want organic, free-range eggs and chickens, they do not come cheap. That is especially true of the less favoured areas like the uplands, the Yorkshire Dales and moors, Cornish common land and so on. These are the things that we like and need, and we should be ready to pay for them rather than either maximising production or indeed simple ownership of large acreage.

So farming subsidy may well change, but I am absolutely confident in thinking that any independent UK government in Westminster will honour it. British farmers need have no fear of Brexit.

Brexit will also give us a moment make a few decisions about how we really want to live, and perhaps for a fundamental rethink of our town and country planning system. Unfettered immigration from the EU has created an unhealthy demand for housing, leading to unaffordable prices for all, urban sprawl across the countryside, especially in the South of England. There are today 200,000 homes in England standing empty, mainly because they are in the wrong place. All kinds of polices over the years have encouraged migration from the North towards the South of the UK, into the already thoroughly congested South of England.

Successive housing and town planning policy has declared it a national duty to provide the housing which we demand, and in the places where we demand it. But is that really right? Does it not create something of a self-fulfilling prophesy? It has for sure resulted in vast swathes of our beloved countryside being buried under housing estates. We tend to live in impenetrable jungles of cul-de-sacs, often remote from our work, our schools, our shops and for that reason making us wholly dependent on our unsustainable cars and the internal combustion engine. That also destroys any real feeling of 'community,' without which our lives are poor little things indeed.

The Prince of Wales conducted an interesting planning experiment at Poundbury in Dorset. He tried to replicate the traditional English village with a genuine variety of different designs of houses arranged not along cul-de-sacs, but on village streets, with car access crucially from behind rather than in front of the houses. Poundbury acknowledges the central importance of the village hall, the shop and church; and sought to provide schools and jobs within walking distance of the homes. Poundbury has had its critics, and no doubt its problems too. It has not necessarily wholly worked as HRH would have liked it. But it may give us a few hints for worthwhile changes to planning policy.

For example, we have a huge shortage in the UK of single-bed high density flats and houses in the middle of towns (a product perhaps of our historic tendency to drift outwards from town centres as we achieve prosperity.) We have always presumed that everyone wants three bedrooms and a double garage and that the further from the centre we can be the better it is. Yet with High Street independent shops in terminal decline thanks both to out of town shopping, and even more so to the Internet, is there not a strong argument in favour of imaginative redevelopment of our high streets and town centres, perhaps especially for the young, and for the elderly, who would actually prefer to live hugger-mugger and closer to shops and transport.

Brexit and the control of our borders and immigration, and new thinking about the size of our sustainable population, and especially where it should live, ought to be a central part of our renewal as an independent nation state. A renewed and refreshed farming and countryside and rural landscape; sustainable and attractive market towns and villages, and renovation of our town centres by more high-density housing may be slightly incidental to Brexit. But it would be a great – if incidental – prize.

19. Britain: Safe and Secure

"Terrorism has no nationality or religion." (Vladimir Putin)

It was the morning after the murder of PC Keith Palmer. As I arrived in Parliament at 7am, I spoke to the police officer on duty at Chancellors Gate. "Did you know Keith?" I asked. "I was on duty with him yesterday morning," he said with a distinct tear in his eye. "Mind how you go now, Sir." The Prime Minister was absolutely right in her magnificent statement later that morning. (As was Margaret Thatcher when she addressed the Party Conference the morning after the Brighton Bomb in 1984.) If we allow terrorist outrages to interfere with our everyday business, then we are letting them win.

I had been having a drink on the Terrace of the House of Commons with Brinkworth farming family, the Collingbornes a few moments before the murderer hit the pedestrians 100 yards away on Westminster Bridge. Thankfully, we had moved just inside to the Terrace Cafeteria and were just sitting down to a plate of British beef when a civilian looking policeman burst in clad in body armour and helmet, balaclava and bristling radios and weapons making him look pretty terrifying. He was screaming and shouting at us to follow him (only slightly hampered by trying to go out the 'In' door which stubbornly refused to budge until I got my fingers around it). All six of us, including young Bede, who at eight years old was as cool as a cucumber, filed quietly up to Central Lobby, where, together with 500 or so other random people we spent the next three hours or so standing up on the hard marble floors.

There was no official announcement of what was going on as the special forces policemen rushed in and out brandishing their weapons, and changing their minds about how to handle this crowd of MPs, peers, staff and visitors. We kept ourselves up to date with events outside on our mobile phones. But, of course no-one knew whether or not this might have been a part of a more concerted Mumbai-style attack perhaps involving several gunmen, some quite possibly inside the building. We kept pretty calm, but some of us understood the risks and worries. We were then evacuated in single file down to Westminster Hall to join a good few hundred others, yet more having been evacuated to the Abbey. Then about 8pm, or five-and-a-half hours after the terrible incident we were allowed to return to our rooms. I was glad to find that all of my team were fit and well, despite my Private Secretary Amy Swash having heard the shots directly outside our office window, and my Chief of Staff, Adam Fico, having witnessed the immediate aftermath. They did not have to come into the office the next morning, nor did my Polar expert, Duncan Depledge. But they were at their desks on time and in good humour (only complaining slightly about the mild hangover caused by the bottle of malt whisky they had found in the

Elizabeth Tower, Palace of Westminster.

room where they took refuge). I salute their resolution.

There is something particularly wicked, and saddening about the killing of a policeman doing his duty. But returning to duty afterwards – as we then all did, and as Keith's colleague on my way in that morning led by example in doing – is absolutely the right thing to do. We will defeat these wicked people. We defeated the IRA, and despite his apparent conversion in recent years, I have to say that I shed no tears at the death of convicted terrorist Martin MacGuiness's funeral the

Police officers guarding the Palace of Westminster.

following morning.

A great deal of nonsense has been talked about the Brexit consequences on law and order and on protection against terrorism. Certainly post-Brexit we will continue to exchange intelligence and cooperate in every way with police forces and intelligence agencies across the Continent of Europe and elsewhere. It would be mad if we did not do so. But cross-border cooperation which is so essential if we are to address cross-border crime and especially multi-national terrorist networks, is by no means dependent on our membership of the EU. There are indeed arguments that that may make it more difficult to ensure continuing intelligence sharing with the US, in particular.

What's more, our departure from the European Court of Justice and the great corpus of European law will give greater primacy to our own courts and Parliament. There is (and should be) a whole swathe of European law which does not apply in the UK, and vice-versa. We will remain (for now) members of the European Court of Human Rights (ECHR), which is answerable to, and whose judges are appointed by, the Council of Europe. (Founded by Churchill in 1946, and including many non-EU states, such as Russia.)

Appeals to the ECJ – in which litigants pray in aid EU law – will end. But appeals to the ECHR, which is largely governed by the European Charter of Human Rights, will, for now, continue. There is a significant debate to be had about the ECHR. It is bogged down under a vast back-log of unheard cases, simply because every citizen with a grievance against their own legal system has an absolute right to appeal to the ECHR on grounds of some 'violation of their human rights' (even if the case bears little relevance to human rights).

Not only that, but there have been a number of rulings from the ECHR, which seem to over-rule British courts and impose decision which are unacceptable in this country. Giving the vote to long-term prisoners, for fear of breaching their human rights is one such example. Parliament and the British courts decided against it only to be over-ruled by the ECHR. The final decision is still pending (like so much else in the ECHR). But if they insist on having their way, there will, I think be an increasing clamour for Britain to leave the ECHR just as we have left the EU, and for rather similar reasons. That, in a way, would be a shame, since the ECHR is actually seeking to impose our high standards of human rights on other member countries whose standards may be much lower.

The reality is that control of our own courts as of our own laws, the right to decide what law is (Parliament) and how it should be applied (the courts up to the Supreme Court – anther Blairite monstrosity) should be the most central of the rights we regain from the EU.

So of course methods must be found to ensure the fair exchange of information about criminals and terrorists. There will always be ways in which our intelligence services and police forces can operate effectively overseas; and vice-versa. But that must not be allowed to undermine that most sacred of all sovereignties – total control of our laws and our courts.

20. Britain: Ethics and Ethos

"Only in Britain could it be thought to be an insult to be 'too clever by half.'"

(John Major)

There is a theme which runs through all of this, and which harks back to our musings in the early chapters of this book about the British character, and in particular what differentiates our character from that of our nearest neighbours – at its closest 22 miles away across the English Channel.

Whether you are talking about defence and foreign affairs, about overseas aid and our pragmatic and reasonable approach to it, about our great parliamentary democracy, our constitutional and legal exemplar to the world. Or about our approach to business and economics post-Brexit, our education and training systems, our way of providing those things which the citizen needs, untrammelled by socialism or state-hating minimalism. Or whether you are talking about schools and hospitals, the countryside, law and order; whichever aspect of the debate over Brexit and our place in the world, there is one constant theme – Britishness.

The reality is that we are different to mainland Europeans. They see 'Europe' as an overwhelmingly important part of their destiny. They view our departure not so much as with distaste as with total incredulity. They simply cannot understand why anyone should disdain their lovely European Club. Why on earth would we want to be on our own? Their approach to Brexit is analogous to anyone in England being bold enough to propose the abolition of the NHS, or the ending of the monarchy. Any such suggestion would be not only obnoxious and unachievable; we would also view it with simple astonishment. How could anyone possibly be proposing the abolition of the NHS? What madness is Republicanism? How could anyone conceivably consider leaving the EU? It's like a kind of theology – a destiny almost.

That difference comes from an extremely fundamental, ancient, complex series of differences between ourselves and our European neighbours. We are islanders. Our history and future are defined and limited by that islandness. We are Protestants – and Max Weber and R. H. Tawney's 'Protestant work ethic' touches on this. Tawney's great work, *Religion and the Rise of Capitalism* argues – in, I hope, not unfairly simple terms – that in the sixteenth and seventeenth centuries in particular, but by extension more recently, Protestantism (sobriety, financial probity, hard work, decency), provided the ethos in which true modern Western capitalism could thrive; and that the Southern European Roman Catholic countries with their hot weather, long holidays, mid-afternoon siestas, alcohol-based social interaction, and the rest was an atmosphere in which hard work, thrift and sober minded determination were undermined and destroyed. It was therefore Germany,

Holland, and especially ultra-protestant England and Calvinist Scotland where sound business instincts thrived. The whole thesis has been the subject of endless academic discussion and criticism for a hundred years and more. But there is without doubt some sense in it.

Generalisations invite criticism based on exceptions to the rule. But as a one-sentence thumbnail portrait of we Brits I would say that we are decent, hardworking, independent minded, capitalistic yet caring dislikers of rules and government. The family remains the corner-stone of our lives; '2.4 children and a Ford Cortina' as we used to say. We dislike snobbism and inverted snobbery alike, we are instinctively conservative with a small 'c'. (In the same way the French are instinctively Socialist, the Italians mildly nihilistic.) And there can be no doubt about it: we consider ourselves to be fundamentally different to every kind of foreigner, especially those who begin at Calais.

It is these differences of character which meant that the European vision including 'an ever-closer union' and incorporating Britain was doomed from the start. The Treaty of Rome almost acknowledges that by calling for Economic and Political Union. Almost no-one believed that the UK would sign up to economic and political union. We played along with the game for a few years, and extracted what benefit we could from it. But those fundamental differences of character and of geography meant from the start that our membership of the EU was doomed.

The British bulldog standing up for all that is best about Britain, and standing against those things about the Continent of Europe should have been enough for the architects of the EU to know that we would never be true Europeans. A glance at the Last Night of the Proms should have told them that.

Rule, Britannia! Britannia, rule the waves!
Britons never, never, never shall be slaves.

When Britain first, at heaven's command,
Arose from out the azure main,
This was the charter of the land,
And Guardian Angels sang this strain:

The nations not so blest as thee
Must, in their turn, to tyrants fall,
While thou shalt flourish great and free:
The dread and envy of them all.

Still more majestic shalt thou rise,
More dreadful from each foreign stroke,
As the loud blast that tears the skies
Serves but to root thy native oak.

Thee haughty tyrants ne'er shall tame;
All their attempts to bend thee down
Will but arouse thy generous flame,
But work their woe and thy renown.

Rule, Britannia! Britannia, rule the waves!
Britons never, never, never shall be slaves.

And Blake's immortal poem:-

And did those feet in ancient time,
Walk upon England's mountains green:
And was the holy Lamb of God,
On England's pleasant pastures seen!

And did the Countenance Divine,
Shine forth upon our clouded hills?
And was Jerusalem builded here,
Among these dark Satanic Mills?

Bring me my Bow of burning gold;
Bring me my Arrows of desire:
Bring me my Spear: O clouds unfold!
Bring me my Chariot of fire!

I will not cease from Mental Fight,
Nor shall my Sword sleep in my hand:
Till we have built Jerusalem,
In England's green & pleasant Land.

Hackneyed clichés they may be, (and in the case of *Jerusalem* mildly nonsensical). But my goodness, anyone who has ever heard English people singing them know how viscerally we feel it. It's not a national anthem; it's not a cheerful song at a good funeral; it's our own little way of laying out in the simplest of terms, napkins and union flags waving, what we feel about ourselves, but which we might well have felt too shy and modest to have articulated otherwise.

Perhaps de Gaulle (maybe subconsciously) knew it, which may be why he delayed our membership of the Common Market for so long in the first place. But a glance at our history shows the same inclination for thousands of years.

We put up with the Roman invader, but never really truly subscribed to his agenda. We fought valiantly against waves of invaders in the Dark Ages, each wave becoming serially as determined as the last to see off the next lot. We preserved our Saxon languages and traditions for a long time after the Normans got here, and at least until we had Anglicised them. We fought Napoleon and the Spanish, the Germans on two separate occasions. The notion that despite all of that we might for some reason of modernism suddenly have become good Europeans, is laughably improbable.

The last heroes of the Battle of Britain survive to this day. That battle symbolises not only our aversion to Nazism and our determination to defeat Adolf Hitler. It's also somehow symbolic of us as a nation. Those little spitfires buzzing about over the English Channel, punching way above their weight, irritating the over-mighty Continentals who were trying to do dreadful things to us. The spirit of cheerful bonhommie in the officers mess each evening populated by people in flying jackets with exaggerated moustaches and a little too much Brylcream up top just waiting for that bell to announce yet another scramble.

RAF pilots ready to scramble.

Who does not smile at Douglas Bader's speech to a primary school class "I had one f....r on my right wing and another on my left, and I had two other f....ers coming up my tail." "Well children," intervened the teacher, "the famous German aeroplane manufacturers were called Fokker." "That's right," said Bader, "but these ones were Messerschmitts." There's something just terribly British about that, mildly self-deprecating.

There's just something about the Battle of Britain which symbolises all that we are as far as the Continent of Europe is concerned, and maybe the Battle of Britain dinners and celebrations continuing to this day should have signified that to them.

"Never in the field of human conflict was so much owed by so many to so few."

I am not ashamed to quote Churchill:

1953 flypast.

"We shall go on to the end. We shall fight in France, we shall fight on the seas and oceans, we shall fight with growing confidence and growing strength in the air. We shall defend our island whatever the cost may be. We shall fight on the beaches, we shall fight on the landing grounds, we shall fight in the fields and in the streets, we shall fight in the hills; we shall never surrender."

"Let us therefore brace ourselves to our duties and so bear ourselves that if the British Empire and its Commonwealth last for a thousand years, men will say 'This was their Finest Hour.'"

"When I warned {the French Government} that Britain would fight on alone whatever they did, their generals told their Prime Minister and his divided cabinet: 'In three weeks England will have her neck rung like a chicken.' Some Chicken! Some neck!"

"I have nothing to offer but blood, toil, tears and sweat."

Now cynics, sophisticated North London wine bar habitues, eaters of guacamole and supporters of Tony Blair's suave citified New Labour will sneer at the use of these famous old quotes from the greatest ever living Englishman. (His grandson, Nicholas Soames tells a tale of how when he was a boy visiting his grandfather at Chartwell, he made his way up through the corridors, guards, private secretaries, and eventually found Winston in bed. He clambered up on to the blankets and turned to his grandfather. "They say that you are the greatest Englishman ever to have lived. Is that true?"

The great man put down his brandy, pulled on his cigar, thought for a moment, turned to the little boy and said:

'Yes. Now bugger off…')

©Jessica Taylor

Churchill wreath laying in Parliament.

The pro-Europeans will laugh at my 'Little Englander' use of Churchill quotes to justify my 'out-dated stance.' They will talk of clichés and hackneyed old musings. Well, let me risk their sneering jibes even further by quoting the great man on the subject of Europe:-

"If Britain must choose between Europe and the open sea, she must always choose the open sea..."

"Where do we stand? We are not members of the European Defence Community, nor do we intend to be merged into a Federal European system. We feel we have a special relationship to both. We are with them, but not of them. We have our own Commonwealth and Empire..."

"In all this urgent work, France and Germany must take the lead together. Great Britain, the British Commonwealth of nations, mighty America, and I trust Soviet Russia must be the friends and sponsors of the new Europe and must champion its right to live and shine."

Academics and historians enjoy an active debate as to whether or not Churchill was a European or a Eurosceptic. And he is frequently 'prayed in aid' of both sides of the argument. I suspect the answer is that at various times in his long life he may well have been various graduations of both. And it would be wrong to use selective quotes as I have done, to justify one argument or the other. They nonetheless give a flavour of my own views of what Europe ought to be like. The fact is that we are different to the Europeans, and some of these quotes from Churchill hint at where that difference lies.

At all events, the fact of the matter as I write in Summer, 2018, is that Article 50 having been triggered, the UK will leave the EU on 31 March 2019. Of that there can be no doubt. What is left for us to debate is what will be the exact method of our going, and what the details of the divorce agreement. What we must now turn our attention to – and it is what this book has tried to do in its own little way – is to what Britain must look like in the post-Brexit world. What are our strengths and our weaknesses, what our peculiarities, what our contribution to the world and to what's left of the EU.

21. Britain in 2050

"This is where I started life. This is where I went to uni. This is where the people I know are. This is my country, and when I put on my Great Britain vest, I'm proud, very proud, that it's my country." (Mo Farah)

There are some things about Britain's 'Greatness,' or lack of it, about which we can be quite clear. We have the natural resources (agriculture, energy, minerals, weather, landscape) to be self-sufficient, and make a useful contribution to the rest of the world.

We have the weather, time zone, geographical location to do so.

We have the historical capacity and ability to do so.

We are the fourth richest country in the world.

We are not only rich, but we also have the capacity to maintain that richness, or make ourselves even richer. As a free and independent trading nation, we will have at last an unfettered ability to buy and sell with other nations around the world. We can make our own trade deals through the World Trade Organisation. Through our mastery of the seas, and our outstanding financial services sector in the City of London, we can once again dominate the world's trading lanes. Not only that, but our universities and schools, our apprenticeships, our world beating engineering and science sectors, our ready availability of finance and a hugely skilled workforce – all of these things and so many more equip us to be second to none in every aspect of business and commerce.

We have the benefits of R. H. Tawney's Protestant work ethic, (hard work, Puritanism, modesty, ambition, thriftiness and all of the virtues which he associated with colder Presbyterian climes in the North of Europe.)

We have the historic and diplomatic positioning to be amongst the greatest. G 20, G 6, UN Security Council, EU, EFTA – you name it we are in it, and at its top table.

We may gripe about it, but we have the military capacity (including crucially our Trident nuclear capability), diplomatic capacity, aid generosity, governmental and parliamentary systems, civil service, media to be the Greatest.

Yet despite all that we seem content with our position towards the top of the second league. We habitually view ourselves as a declining nation. We think of the Far East, the BRIC nations as being the fast-expanding hope of the next century. We are poor old Britain stuck in a rain-sodden geographic extremity, watching the rest of the world advance as we teeter along on our ancient bicycles.

It's partly natural modesty, partly sentimental nostalgia for days of former greatness, which we feel ill-equipped to repeat; it's partly the perfectly accurate realisation that others have cheaper labour and better natural resources than we. But above all else largely it comes from our natural tendency to love talking ourselves down. The same mildly negative frame of mind applies to our view of the weather ("It's nice, but can only get wet later"), to sport ("They did well, but can they really keep up that pace?") to material success ("What's he done to earn that Rolls Royce, that big house?") and to the economy ("Surprise figures announced this morning show a further reduction in unemployment, further increase in growth. Economists commented that it was despite Brexit, and may just be a temporary blip").

The Americans are positive optimistic and boastful. We tend to be miserable, negative and pessimistic. But that is not how we achieved greatness. In those days we knew we were the best and set about proving it to the world.

Today's reality is that we have the intellectual, economic, military, diplomatic and every other resource necessary to be a truly Great Nation. We need to be clear about our aims and our capacities, and there are tweaks needed to our diplomatic mission, military and economic goals.

But by far the biggest change necessary is in how we see ourselves. We need to shake off our post-imperialist embarassments; we need to free ourselves of the bureaucratic shackles of the European Union; we need to aim for the best, to talk ourselves up; to punch above our weight, walk tall and carry our heads high with the greatest in the world.

We may never be as rich as China or America; we may not match Brazil's agricultural wealth, nor Russia's vast natural resources. We may not have as many people as China or India, nor as much cheap manufacturing labour.

But we have the imagination, the intelligence, the innate material abilities to make ourselves great again. We need not be cowering rain-soaked, cabbage-eating third raters. We can, and we must, once again be a truly Great Britain. Brexit gives us that opportunity.